Adult Sibling Rivalry

Adult Sibling Rivalry

Understanding the Legacy of Childhood

Dr. Jane Greer
with
Edward Myers

CROWN PUBLISHERS, INC., NEW YORK

Copyright © 1992 by Dr. Jane Greer

Published by Crown Publishers, Inc., 201 East 50th Street, New York, New York
10022. Member of the Crown Publishing Group.

CROWN is a trademark of Crown Publishers, Inc.

Manufactured in the United States of America

Library of Congress Cataloging-in-Publication Data
Greer, Jane, 1951–
Adult sibling rivalry : understanding the legacy of childhood /
Jane Greer,with Edward Myers.—1st ed.
p.   cm.
Includes bibliographical references and index.
1. Sibling rivalry. 2. Adulthood—Psychological aspects.
I. Myers, Edward, 1950– . II. Title.
BF723.S43G74   1992   91-42687
155.6′4—dc20   CIP

Designed by Leonard Henderson

ISBN 0-517-58276-7

10 9 8 7 6 5 4 3 2 1

First Edition

To my brother
For all we've shared together

Contents

Contents

Author's Note

As a psychotherapist, I consider it my first priority to safeguard the confidentiality of my patients and interview subjects. In the interest of protecting their privacy, I have changed the names of all persons mentioned in the book, except the psychologists and other theorists quoted. I have also altered the details of people's lives—their professions, family backgrounds, and other potentially identifying circumstances. In most instances, the examples are composites of two or three persons used to obscure their identities and to clarify the relevant issues. Any similarities between the anecdotes I present and any actual person, living or dead, is entirely coincidental.

This book is not intended as a substitute for psychotherapy with a qualified professional.

Introduction:
It's All Relative

It's no secret that family life includes a measure of conflict; even so, many people are astonished by the intensity and durability of their conflicts with relatives. And among the relatives who cause the most astonishment are siblings.

I hear many people express confusion, exasperation, or sadness about relationships with their sisters and brothers. They want to get along with their siblings but end up in conflict. They're frustrated by being related yet unable to relate to them. They want to find common ground but often find differences and misunderstandings instead. They want to share the warmth of love and mutual supportiveness but feel the chill of unease, anger, or resentment. They puzzle over how (as one woman put it) "we're all adults now, yet my sisters and I squabble just like we did as kids" or, as one of my patients said, "No matter how much we talk, my brother and I can't seem to communicate. We just don't understand each other."

Implicit in these laments is a belief that sibling conflict is a feature solely of childhood. It is (or ought to be) a thing of the past by the time we become adults and face similar life events: working, getting married, and starting families. The powerful factors that once separated us soon diminish; differences in our ages, roles, and developmental stages become far less significant than when we were children. Yet despite our expectations that we'll now get along, we still end up in conflict. Hence our bafflement, anger, and sadness when misunderstandings multiply and battles rage. How come we end up arguing? Hasn't our sibling rivalry ended?

In fact, sibling rivalry isn't confined to childhood. It originates there, but its legacies are numerous and powerful, and they often linger for decades. The feelings and roles we experienced as children follow us not just into youth but into middle age and even old age—clear to the end of our days. Indeed, these feelings and roles do more than follow: they influence us and limit us; they inspire us and motivate us; they exhaust us and demoralize us; they affect us in a thousand intricate and often contradictory ways; they entangle us for the rest of our lives. Precisely because these legacies run so far back—for many people, all the way to birth—they have an extraordinary grip on our thoughts, emotions, and behaviors: in short, on who we are.

Our adult sibling conflicts often derive from the "child" still deep inside us—a vestige of the child who once loved, resented, was jealous of, admired, fought with, longed for, was tormented by, and received affection from sisters and brothers. This is the child who felt a distance separating him or her from siblings; who envied an older sister's athletic prowess; who resented a younger brother's academic success. As we reach womanhood or manhood, we tend to imagine that we're leaving behind the child we were. We assume that our negative feelings toward our siblings will simply disappear.

To some extent we *do* leave the child behind. And in a sense our negative feelings *do* disappear. But they don't really go away; they just take on a new guise. They begin to show up in our love relationships, our work relationships, and our friendships. The effects are so subtle that most of us don't even realize that the forces of siblinghood are at work here. While it is taken for granted that our parents influence us as we grow and develop, it is seldom acknowledged how strongly our siblings affect how we see and feel about ourselves.

Both the positive and the negative experiences of siblinghood linger for a lifetime. This is especially true for the negative feelings of resentment, envy, and jealousy that often result from being compared with siblings and feeling that we fall short of them.

As a psychotherapist, I've watched dozens of people struggle with "sibling issues," and over the years I've noted which of these issues cause the most trouble and what sorts of responses seem to help resolve them. For this reason, *Adult Sibling Rivalry* is a book for all adults who have endured the experience of sibling rivalry as children and now find themselves grappling with the array of problems entailed in getting along with brothers and sisters as grown-ups—from commonplace problems like dealing with in-laws, holidays, and family conflicts to more acute problems that continue to influence our behavior and wreak havoc. Furthermore, this book is about the powerful impact that relationships have on adults' current interactions with other people at work, in marriage, or in other realms of life. Specifically, it concerns how sibling rivalry—a normal part of growing up in a family—often profoundly influences our perceptions, beliefs, feelings, memories, and actions throughout our lifetimes.

What are some of the problems that siblings experience during adulthood? They can be relatively mild, garden-variety difficulties of the sorts that most sisters and brothers confront, or they can be more severe problems.

Here are some of the many questions that typify brothers and sisters trying to get along:

- My sister is coming in for a week, but we end up arguing because she always tells me what to do. How do I deal with her?

- My brother is moving to California to become a bartender. I'm worried about this, and I want to talk with him, but I don't know what to say without sounding too controlling.

- My boyfriend's older brother just split up with his wife and showed up at our place. He wants to stay with us. How do we deal with him?

- My sister always changes her plans. I had plans to go to a movie with her, but she backed out at the last minute when something better came along. I feel unimportant. What should I do?

- My sister can't seem to say a word that doesn't criticize or humiliate me. What should I tell her?

- Why is my sister so detached from our family? We all feel bad when she doesn't come to family events. What should we do?

- I can't stand being with my husband and his brother when they're together. They're so competitive. Where does this come from?

- My husband dislikes my brother-in-law, and this is straining my relationship with my sister. What do I do?

This list could go on and on. If you scratch the surface of any adult who has a brother or sister, he or she will have a list of complaints or frustrations about relating to siblings.

All these questions show people groping for ways to deal with their brothers and sisters, to get along with them, to understand them. This sense of groping is distressingly common. Why? Because no one teaches us what we should or shouldn't *do* as siblings. As a result, siblinghood is not only a different experience for each of us but often a confusing experience as well. One result is that most of us strive to be a good brother or sister—that is, we try to attain what I call the ideal of the Good-Enough Sibling—a goal that causes great frustration precisely because it is so undefined and open-ended. Evaluating your ideal of siblinghood—your sense of what it means to be a Good-Enough Sibling—means determining specifically what siblinghood entails for you. After all, each sibling relationship is unique; what one person will do for her sister or brother, another would never consider. Hence you need to reflect on your ideal of siblinghood to formulate legitimate expectations of yourself and your brothers and sisters.

What about more intense, complex, and disruptive problems? What if you feel burdened by a brother's or sister's troubles?

Consider Sally, who feels responsible time after time for rescuing her sister Marcia whenever she gets fired or runs out of money. Sally provides Marcia's only safety net. Although she wants to help, Sally feels exhausted by her sister's constant troubles—and by her own sense of obligation to help. Is she her sister's keeper? How can she find a balance between Marcia's needs and her own? Sally is what I call the Supersibling: one who feels an unending and often burdensome commitment to helping, rescuing, or bailing out a sister or brother.

And what about sibling relationships that are plagued with anger and periodically deteriorate into complete silence—a sibling "cold war"? For example, Emily doesn't know what she's done, but her brother John will have nothing to do with her. Emily feels judged, maligned, and persecuted: when Emily phones her brother, John says, "I don't want to talk with you," and hangs up. Emily doesn't know what to do about this inexplicable impasse.

What if you feel that your sibling has wronged you terribly? Here's an example: Greg and his brother Larry are in pretty close contact with each other, but tensions run fast and strong below the surface. Some time ago, the brothers decided to buy a car for their father. Each put down half the money. However, Larry was the only one who signed the contract. When the time came to sell the car, Larry cheated Greg out of his share of the profit. Greg felt angry but shrugged it off: "Well, that's just my brother! You take the good qualities with the bad." Meanwhile, Greg's personal life is in chaos. He's engaged in an ongoing battle with his wife. Finances are a divisive issue; Greg even accuses his wife of trying to take advantage of him. What's going on here? Is it possible that Greg's unresolved conflicts with his brother are "haunting" his marriage and other relationships?

What's happening is what I call the Invisible Sibling: sibling strife taking place with others rather than directly with sisters and brothers. People don't realize how compelling their relationships with siblings are, and how deep the attachments run. It's not unusual to find people establishing brotherly or sisterly attachments to others in their life. The Invisible Sibling can take the form of partner, boss, best friend— even a total stranger—because there is a tremendous desire to heal unresolved sibling conflicts.

By looking at these sibling phenomena, you can *see* things in a clearer and more insightful manner, so that you can begin to develop what I call your I-power—self-awareness and self-confidence—which will enable you to assert yourself. From there you can truly shape the kinds of relationships you want to have—not only with brothers and sisters but with all those who matter to you.

Adult Sibling Rivalry covers many topics. While you may not find your particular situation here, you may discover that the techniques and skills described are applicable to your own experiences.

Ultimately, this is the goal: if you can understand sibling rivalry and its long-term effects, you can learn to deal better with the old emotional wounds that sibling rivalry may have caused and that remain alive and troublesome in the here and now. Then you can not only start to heal the wounds but also move toward the kinds of sibling relationships you want.

Part One

How Did We End Up Like This?

———

1

Siblinghood Is Powerful

At the time I got married, my sister was really angry at me.
She always thought I got more than she did. This was nothing
new; she'd always felt this way. But now she thought it was
true for my wedding, too. Here I was beginning a new marriage with someone who was very loving and caring and solid,
while she had just gotten married and was now getting separated from someone who was an alcoholic. So around the
wedding there were already problems.

She showed up so underdressed! She wore the ugliest dress
that she could possibly find in her closet. No makeup. Nothing. Everybody else was decked out. It was as if everyone else
had been in black tie and she showed up in gym shorts!
That's the only way I can describe the dissonance between
how she was dressed and everyone else. She thought this
would reflect on me—but all it did was reflect on her!

What I then had to deal with was explaining to three sets
of cousins why she was angry with me. I wouldn't reveal the
family secrets. So I got caught in a bind. She was saying,
"Look at me, she's got everything! I've got a miserable life!
I have no job, I'm living on alimony!" You'd think she was
talking about me as if we were six years old.

—Vicky

I avoid my younger sister now but am always pleasant when we talk. I have been told by several people that no one—not even my younger sister herself—suspects that I don't get along with her. In fact, she often calls for advice on restaurants or business. I'm pleasant but I don't go out of my way to be nice to her. But I don't antagonize her because it's not worth the aggravation of her outbursts.

One day I found out that my father's prostate cancer biopsy was positive, and that the cancer had spread through his bloodstream. Only my mother and I knew this information. That night, I attended an annual Christmas party at my younger sister's. She asked me if I'd found out anything about the tests. I asked if she'd like to know now or later. She said now—at the party. But when I told her, she got furious and said she wouldn't forgive me for ruining her party.

—Patty

Only now can I say I've started getting over how my brother emotionally abused me. He took every opportunity to hassle me for everything and anything I did. To this day, I can't stand talking to him because he always has to be right—at my expense. He doesn't realize how much he destroyed my self-esteem and confidence. Everything he is, I want to be exactly the opposite. I am as loyal and supportive as I can be to people I care about.

—Kevin

Unless you are an only child, you have been influenced by having grown up among brothers and sisters. Moreover, what you experienced in relation to your siblings still affects your perception of who you are, what you want, and how you see the world. Even if your direct interaction with your siblings ceased when you became an adult, the time you spent with them has changed you forever. More than that: it has *shaped* you. For siblinghood is one of the fundamental formative aspects of your life, and it will partially determine whether you pursue your interests and relationships with or without a sense of choice in obtaining what you want.

Like other potentially rewarding experiences—marriage, parenthood, or work—siblinghood may be complex, ambiguous, confusing, and difficult: an experience that often requires close attention and effort to make it rewarding. The realities of our individual relationships are far messier than our idealized images of them. Siblinghood isn't a single, consistent experience; rather, it's continually changing, even when it seems most static. Siblinghood is partly what you've been given (the family you were born into) and partly what you extract from the situation. That is, siblinghood is partly what it is and partly what you make of it. Some aspects of your situation are beyond your control. You can't decide to have different parents; you can't go back and have different brothers and sisters. However, you can take hold of your past experiences, remember events more fully, understand them better, and grasp causes and effects; you can reach new insights about the family dynamics that influenced you.

Whether positive, negative, or mixed, the experience of siblinghood is powerful—probably more powerful than you wish to admit. But as with other determinants of your identity, siblinghood is an experience that you can't harness without first understanding the sources of its power.

And the most significant source of power in siblinghood is sibling rivalry.

Watch baby animals of most mammalian species, and you will see sibling rivalry in action. Newborn puppies will claw past one another to reach their mother's teats; kittens will struggle to nestle against their mother for warmth and safety; young monkeys will squabble for maternal attention, contact, and food. In animals such as these, sibling rivalry is a side effect of basic biological drives for physical and emotional sustenance.

Sibling rivalry among human children is more complex, but it serves similar purposes. Sisters and brothers vie not only for their parents' physical care but for their love, attention, approval, intellectual stimulation, and guidance. Such competition is simply part of being human. Sibling rivalry does not mean that children are too aggressive or demanding, or that parents are insufficiently nurturing; even the children of the most attentive, experienced, affectionate parents will compete with one another. Sibling rivalry isn't an intrinsically negative force. It can take all sorts of positive forms. It's a way for children to learn assertiveness; it's also a testing ground for coping with the wider world; it even provides the setting for sisters and brothers to master cooperation. Sibling rivalry is in essence a survival mechanism—a means by which children try to obtain a fair share of parental resources.

Given its fundamental nature and intensity, however, sibling rivalry exerts enormous pressures in a family. Under ideal circumstances, it assists in the distribution of material and emotional "goods." Under other (sometimes unhealthy) circumstances, it's a divisive, even destructive force. (One small boy's earliest spoken sentence was "No fair!"—a plaintive battle cry in a family where he felt perpetually deprived of his share of the parents' and siblings' attentions.) Either way, sibling rivalry is unquestionably the most powerful dynamic among sisters and brothers while they are growing up. Fully as significant, however, and often more damaging, is the fact that sibling rivalry lives on long after childhood. Even if brothers and sisters have outwardly amicable relations—or little or no contact at all—the old rivalries keep influencing their attitudes not only toward one another but toward many other people as well.

Why is sibling rivalry so important? The main reason is that, in both its positive and its negative forms, sibling rivalry powerfully influences the development of one's sense of identity. Perhaps the strongest aspect of sibling rivalry is its effect on the desire to be the same as brothers and sisters, and the simultaneous desire to be different from them. In addition to the parents' contributions, this is an essential ingredient in how children establish their identities.

Watch any two very young siblings together—let's say a one-year-old and a three-year-old—and you'll generally see the younger child imitate the older one. Something within prompts children to imitate, to emulate, to share certain characteristics with their siblings. This is especially conspicuous in early childhood. Generally called identification, it's the psychological process by which you take on another person's traits to form part of your own personality. This process propels children to acquire characteristics not only from their parents but from their siblings as well.

Yet even as they strive for similarity with members of their family, children work hard to define themselves as different. This effort is most conspicuous during adolescence, but it is apparent earlier as well. You probably had the experience during childhood of liking something—a certain sport, a kind of music, a style of clothing—only to discover that Big Sister or Little Brother had defiled it with her or his own appreciation, prompting you to shift your enthusiasm to something else. This push toward being different from one's siblings is as normal as the pull toward being the same.

Generally speaking, neither the desire to be "just like" nor the urge to be "nothing like" one's sisters or brothers is a problem unless it becomes unbalanced. If your desire to be similar or different is so strong that you forfeit choice, it can be troublesome. That is, you might strive to resemble a sibling despite your unique abilities, characteristics, and interests; or you might work hard to be different from a sister or brother, repressing valuable traits and talents that happen to resemble your sibling's.

One way that wanting to differ from siblings can go awry is in an attitude I call the occupied zone. Let's say your sister is good at school; academics is the zone she occupies. That's her turf, so you stay clear. Why? Because staying clear diminishes envy, jealousy, and rivalry, thus reducing the risk of conflict. Yet the cost is often great in restricting your personal or professional development. For example, Phoebe never understood why she was uncomfortable in social situations. "My sister was the cute one with boyfriends, and I was the studious one who had a problem with her weight. I shut down with her to avoid getting hurt and feeling I wasn't as good as her. I really was attractive, but the family roles were set at a young age." This account illustrates how Phoebe's sister had occupied the zone of attractiveness. While Phoebe excelled in academics, she felt a need to relinquish territory in the social realm. But giving up that sphere ultimately left her feeling negative about herself.

Then there's Richard and his interactions with his brother Warren. "I had a feeling as I was growing up that in some ways I thought I was my parents' favorite—at least vis-à-vis Warren. I'm not sure why. I'm not sure if every child feels that, or if every child feels the opposite. He chose very different things in life. He chose music, and he chose that pretty early—junior high school, or around then. He was in all the bands he could find. And I was, too, but for me it was just a diversion. I've wondered whether that was deliberate on his part to avoid competition, to distinguish himself. Academics was part of my identity as a kid. I did well in school, and I liked knowing that I did well in school. I felt good about that, and I think my parents felt good about it. So my guess now might be that he either didn't want to try to compete with that or didn't think he *could* compete with that; so he chose music instead." Richard had occupied the zone of academics; Warren therefore felt a need to occupy the zone of artistic pursuits—in this case, music—to mark off his personal turf.

Parents may unwittingly strengthen these occupied zones by making comparisons between their children, which may lead in turn to their showing favoritism or preferential treatment. "Sandra is very verbal," a father says, "but Josh is more artistic." Or a mother states, "Jacqueline seems much shier than her sister." Such comparisons are often well-intentioned, but, well-intentioned or not, they may pigeonhole children in roles that don't fit them. Sometimes quirks or bad habits are exaggerated and become encompassing roles. For instance, Jon tended to be slower and less energetic than his brother Bill. Whereas Bill would quickly complete any task his parents assigned him, Jon would stall when asked to do something, then take his time completing it. Within a short time, Jon's parents had tagged him the Lazy One; in an even shorter time, Jon started feeling bad about himself.

In the face of comparison, your brother's or sister's favorable "rating" means (in your eyes) that he or she has more love. For instance, Melissa recalls that her parents often compared her grades with her sister Kate's. Melissa tended to feel that her parents cherished Kate more because she was so smart. Every comparison seemed like an outpouring of love for Kate—proof to Melissa that she was less loved.

Sibling rivalry influences your identity by affecting how good or bad you feel about yourself—that is, your self-esteem. A child who sees her sibling get more of Mom's and Dad's attention may equate "She gets more attention" with "She's worth more than I am." If she has something that you don't, she's more valued. If she is more valued, you're less valued. If she is worth more to your parents (in your eyes), then you're worth less to them. Unfortunately, children often equate feeling "worth less" to their parents (when compared with their siblings) with feeling "worthless" about themselves. In the dynamic of sibling rivalry, such feelings often create a hollow place that needs to be filled.

How does this experience of valuation affect you in the long run? It's not hard to guess. If as a child you felt that you were worth less than your siblings, you may recall this feeling and resent it years after leaving home. (It's also possible that you won't remember it but will *still* be influenced by what happened.) Many people seek ways of redressing their grievances. In some cases they seek out their siblings to settle the score. Sibling competitiveness over who has the best job, income, house, marriage, or children also reflects this kind of effort. They look to measure their success against that of their siblings; in short, their sense of success is contingent on their siblings' success.

For example, Joe always resented his younger brother Mike for getting so much attention from their parents when they were children. He never understood what his brother possessed that Joe himself seemed to lack. As an adult, Joe found it important to have more money than Mike because Mike had always "gotten the better end of things" when they were boys. Tangible goods—a house, a car, or money in the bank—can thus become a vehicle for sisters and brothers to assert themselves and declare their value. The feeling of having been "one under" as a child fuels their desire to be "one up on" their siblings in adulthood. In other instances, people attempt to heal these old wounds by craving affection or approval from friends, lovers, or even employers and co-workers.

In short, soothing the wounds of sibling rivalry becomes a means for feeling better about oneself. Beating someone in a competition produces a momentary sense of worth. However, victory of this sort often doesn't provide that *internal* sense of self-worth people feel they've lost or never had. This is why many competitive people achieve their goals yet still end up feeling that the "prizes"— material possessions, power, status—aren't enough.

Negative feelings about yourself and your worth can be aggravated further in the present when a sibling still directs or controls your life. If you ask people to tell you their key gripe about sisters or brothers, you'll invariably hear about disapproval, sometimes coupled with interference. What they're doing with their lives—who they're marrying, how they're running their business, even how they're decorating their home—has not received their sister's or brother's approval. Sometimes siblings will do more than negate your actions by their disapproval or simple lack of acknowledgment; they may still be controlling your life or "trying to help." The message you hear from them is "You can't do it right; you can't do it without *me*." So even if the help comes from good intentions—"for your own good"—it can inadvertently chisel away at your self-esteem and independence.

Your experiences of being just like or different from your sisters and brothers, and your feelings about your merits, talents, and worth, add up to influence your sense of identity. Your identity is also affected by your general place in the family system. Who you are is directly connected to who your sister or brother is. As the American psychologists Stephen Bank and Michael Kahn have stated in their book *The Sibling Bond,* "The lifelong quest for a secure personal identity is inextricably woven into that of one's siblings."

2

Take Your Seat

Human beings are territorial. In any classroom most students will choose the same seat day after day. Commuters arriving at work will often argue with anyone who takes their assigned parking space. In psychotherapy groups, patients may insist on sitting in "their" chairs despite possible conflicts with other members of the group. Even toddlers in a sandbox will fuss if other tots intrude on their favorite spot.

Territoriality is simply part of being alive. It's a way of feeling safe and comfortable. By identifying with a physical object or place, people gain a sense of security and stability. Whether in a classroom, a parking lot, a therapist's office, or a sandbox, staking out our territory is one of the ways we deal with life.

The same holds true at the family table. In most families, each person has a seat. The layout may or may not consist of Dad at the head, Mom at the far end, and the kids on either side; families come up with all sorts of arrangements to suit their purposes. What seems consistent, however, is that each family member has a little piece of personal territory at the table: a special seat. In fact, there are few places where seats are more rigidly assigned.

This happens to some extent as a matter of habit. A customary seat can allow a reassuring sense of belonging. However, the table can also reveal each member's place in the family. Who sits next to Father? Who sits next to Mother? Who sits in a place hinting at more domestic responsibility—perhaps nearest the kitchen? Who sits in a place that suggests *less* responsibility—perhaps at the far corner?

To put it bluntly: each seat may come with a set of expectations that have shaped (and continue to shape) your family role. Your seat at the family table is merely an outward sign of where your family has placed you or, at times, where you've placed yourself in the family. And more often than not each member of the family—parents and siblings alike—contributes to keeping you in your seat.

Roles are guidelines for socially appropriate behavior. They are patterns of expectation for how we live our lives. They are not necessarily explicit. That is, instead of being told what to do in words, we are told in nonverbal ways—with a disapproving glance, a shake of the head, a frown, a smile. Even if expectations are not communicated outright, however, the roles they shape are powerful. And seats are one way that roles are represented in the family.

Most people end up with multiple roles as a result of these dynamics. One role is gender—that is, being male or female—with strong (though now changing) expectations about masculine and feminine behavior. Another role is being a daughter or a son. Another is being a sister or a brother. Yet another is being an only child, which has its own expectations for involvement in a family. Friend, student, worker, and spouse are four more roles that may have a strong place in our lives as we grow older.

As discussed in Chapter 1, forces such as sibling rivalry, parental expectations, and the similarities and differences that you perceive between yourself and your family members influence both your individual identity and your identity in your family. You absorb into your personality certain skills, traits, and attitudes. These gradually become consistent enough to seem like guiding lights for your behavior. Such attributes end up seeming like "you." They are in part the roles you have acquired.

Although roles are often shaped by the people we live with, we sometimes make a choice on some level to go along with how we have been defined. Sometimes we go along with a role because it provides a sense of where we fit into the family, sometimes because the forces defining us are too powerful to resist, sometimes because we find the role itself flattering and positive, and sometimes because we don't know how to manage the anger we feel about our role. Sometimes we even go along out of spite: "If that's what they think I am, then that's what I'll be!" But sometimes we go along because these roles have shaped us so fully that we are unaware of the extent of their influence. Acquiescence at least allows a sense of guidance, since no one is likely to tell you what to be in more explicit terms.

Of course, there's lots of advice—not to mention interminable requests, commands, hints, veiled and not-so-veiled threats, and all sorts of contradictory suggestions from friends, relatives, teachers, and the whole cast of characters making up our personal drama. But ultimately *we* are the ones who sort out all these bits of information and assemble a sense of who we are and where we fit in the world. *We* have to conjure our own vision of what it means to be a good daughter or son, sister or brother, wife or husband, mother or father. *We* have to juggle all our roles and their often conflicting expectations to build a sense of identity. In addition, we sometimes limit how much of our own personalities we express to meet the different roles we are expected to assume. This is why we may end up feeling that there isn't a good "fit" between who we are and the roles we have taken on.

Roles serve many purposes, not least organizing what might otherwise be domestic chaos. Roles contribute a sense of order to the family. They provide a means for people to know where they belong in family activities. Your role is also the part you play in the family. In this sense, the family is a stage, and your role is part of a drama. By complex and often unconscious processes, family members cast one another in different roles.

Perhaps it's inevitable that one child gets pegged one way, a second in another way, a third in still another. It's hard for parents not to perceive their children's quirks and foibles; it's hard not to categorize these traits to simplify the complexity of family life. Your parents' marital relationship, their relationships with their siblings, your place in the order of birth, your gender, and several other factors all contribute to how you interact with your family. For the most part, this isn't problematic. Roles can, in fact, be helpful in shaping personality and identity. The problem is that roles all too often can become polarized or rigid. Ideally, roles are flexible, allowing room for people to change and grow; in reality, roles are often too rigid and restrict people from the breadth or depth of experience that they might attain. Then they limit rather than encourage growth and change. Just as actors sometimes find themselves "typecast"— pegged in one role to the exclusion of all others—members of a family can become trapped in a role. One kid is the good one, the other is bad. One is bright, one is slow, one is just average. One kid is a charmer, the other is a wallflower. There's always a risk of ending up in a rigid role and not being able to escape. Whether roles serve positive or negative purposes—and most serve both—they offer structure and shape to experience. This holds true as much for siblinghood as for other relationships in the family.

Often, sisters and brothers puzzle over how different they are from one another despite coming from the same family. For instance, Betty has an older sister whom she has admired and looked up to her whole life. Now thirty-seven, Betty speaks wistfully of the differences between herself and her sister: "Tobi is so strong. She can handle all sorts of things that I can't. I don't understand it—we come from the same family." Similarly, Lois—the oldest of three, with one sister and one brother—doesn't understand why her younger sister seems so smart, wise, and confident. "Did she somehow start out with more than I did?" Lois asks.

In fact, although you were raised in the same family, your experience of family life was dramatically different from that of your brothers and sisters. Each child is born into a different marital environment. When you were born, how old were your parents? How long had they been married? How stable was their marriage? Where were they in their careers? Were they physically healthy? Were they first-time or experienced parents? Each of these situations influenced your parents' relationship and how they responded to you at the time of your birth and during your childhood. Their physical, emotional, marital, and financial circumstances combined to create your family environment.

Moreover, these factors contributed to the level of stress they experienced and how well they got along. On the one hand, parents may be able to work well together and model cooperative behavior for their children. On the other hand, their ways of dealing with stress may include fighting and attacking each other, which in turn dramatically increases sibling rivalry. When parents argue, there are two likely results: they model negative or destructive behavior for their children; and they are less apt to intervene when their children behave in similar ways.

In addition, most children find their parents' marital conflicts stressful. Unable to direct their anxiety back toward their parents, the siblings displace hostile or angry emotions onto one another, which also increases sibling rivalry. Consider how Julie interacted with her older sister: "My parents never did anything about our conflicts; they just let her treat me terribly. I hated her and how she treated me."

If your parents had sisters and brothers, their own experiences as siblings also had a major effect on how they raised you. How your mother and father got along with their sisters or brothers (and how each of them gets along with them now) influenced (and still influences) your relationships with your siblings.

What your parents experienced with their own brothers and sisters partially defined their sense of siblinghood. This influenced how they raised you and your brothers and sisters, thus affecting your own sense of siblinghood. For instance, Bruce and his brother have fought bitterly since childhood. His brother constantly criticizes Bruce. Whenever they can disagree, they do. Recently, in therapy, I asked Bruce about his parents' sibling relationships. He had never thought about them before but was soon considering the rivalry between his father and his uncle. He came to realize that the way his father got along with his own brother had affected the way their father treated Bruce and his brother, and thus had significantly influenced their relationship.

For an indication of how dramatically parents' sibling relationships can affect their children, consider the effect of names. Keith was named after his mother's brother—an erratic, unstable man regarded throughout the family as the Crazy One. As it happened, Keith's father couldn't stand his brother-in-law. Inheriting this man's name burdened Keith with the legacy of their conflict. Keith felt constantly scapegoated by his father, though it took him years to understand that his name made him a fill-in for the hated brother-in-law and that this was one of the reasons Keith's father favored his other son.

Another example: Neil's parents named him after his mother's favorite brother, who had been killed during World War II at the age of thirty-four. Because his death was still so painful to Neil's mother, she couldn't stand to use her brother's name. Neil ended up with the nickname Butch. In addition to being unable to use his own name, Neil carried both the honor and the burden of his revered uncle's image. Part of this burden was Neil's fear that he too would die at the age of thirty-four. He didn't, but this fear took a toll anyway.

Your parents may also have had "unfinished business" with their own siblings. The sibling bond is often difficult for people to detect as an influence on their behavior—especially during adulthood. When people move into their own adult family roles, they often think that the impact of their sibling relationships has diminished or ceased. However, physical distance does not equal psychological separation. On the contrary: the sibling bond often remains intensely powerful even when people move great distances and see their brothers and sisters infrequently. As a matter of fact, it's all the more powerful precisely because the influence is unseen. For this reason, your parents' unresolved feelings about their brothers and sisters can affect their relationships with you without either you or your parents noticing.

Debbie illustrates this issue. She had gotten along badly with her sister, Kathleen, ever since they were children. Kathleen belittled Debbie and took every opportunity to undercut her self-confidence. Now Debbie catches herself involuntarily belittling her own daughter despite her desire to be supportive and loving. Debbie may well be replicating her own sibling relationship in her behavior toward her daughter.

Alternatively, Roger, who as a child felt overpowered by a dominant sibling, now finds himself dominated by his son. He learned to behave in a passive way as a child coping with a demanding brother; now he struggles against the same behavioral patterns even though his "opponent" is decades younger.

The influences of parents' sibling experiences can take many forms. The most common are those in which parents consciously or unconsciously expect family interactions to resemble what they experienced; and, alternatively, those in which parents strive to *avoid* a resemblance to what happened in the past. In the first instance, the parents may end up reliving their sibling conflicts through their own children. In the second, the parents, having experienced one set of circumstances during childhood, want something very different as they raise their own children. Either way, the risk is that the parents will set the stage and assign roles without understanding the source of what they're doing.

Your place in the order of birth also has a great deal to do with how your parents raised you. Moreover, whether you're the oldest, youngest, or a middle child plays a large part in shaping the family role you acquire. The accident of birth casts you in a role that includes expectations for your place in the family. These expectations shape attitudes, skills, and personality traits, which in turn shape behaviors—sharing, manipulating, controlling, demanding, helping, and supporting other family members. Your place in the order of birth thrusts you into a family setting that then cultivates one or more attitudes, skills, and traits.

Oldest children—the firstborn—often inherit their parents' high expectations, especially of being responsible and sharing. As a result, they are often leaders, and many exhibit an unusually strong sense of generosity. However, there may be a negative undercurrent for them as well: uncertainty about what they can keep for themselves. Anita, for instance, frequently heard her mother tell her, "You're selfish," when she refused to share with her siblings. Consequently, Anita learned to share clothing, toys, and many other things—but never learned to deal with her guilt about holding on to things for herself.

Firstborns, unlike children born later, have a period of exclusivity with their parents. This time offers these children an opportunity to identify with their parents. As a result, they may aspire to follow in their parents' career footsteps. This identification may carry them into roles of prominence and success. They are often the favorite children because there was so much excitement about their arrival. They gain importance simply by having shown up. But there is a repercussion: a psychological jolt when another child arrives and ends the period of exclusivity.

Both pressures to share and age can lead to a quasi-parental role for the firstborn—at times without the power that accompanies parenthood. Valerie describes her role as her brothers' and sister's babysitter in these terms: "Every weekend my parents would have an engagement of some sort. If I had a date, I was allowed to go out; but this was a fairly safe thing because I was not dating regularly. They could pretty much count on me. I'd be like any baby-sitter—except that there was so much going on in terms of power struggles. I don't think this would have happened with an unrelated baby-sitter. If you give her any trouble, you're going to have a pretty severe talk with your parents. But if you have a captive baby-sitter, she's got to put up with whatever the kids do. If I'd used any kind of discipline, then my parents would learn I did this. And only my parents were allowed to do that sort of thing." In short, the responsibility invested in the oldest sibling can be a double-edged sword. The oldest may end up with what seems a lot of power but in reality may be little more than a figurehead.

For some firstborns, the impact of birth order carries over into adulthood. While the exclusive relationship with his parents is special and often instills confidence, the firstborn experiences the most severe sibling shock when the next child is born. The second child and every child thereafter arrives with one or more siblings already on the scene. The firstborn, however, feels the jolt of the transition from an exclusive relationship with the parents to a shared one, and with it a feeling of being displaced. That jolt can reverberate throughout the rest of the firstborn's life.

There may be other factors as well. For instance, some firstborns may wind up feeling a bit like guinea pigs. Their parents "practiced" on them. They were stricter, more demanding, less confident. The oldest may also feel that he or she had to battle for turf and privileges; the younger siblings invaded the territory the firstborn had staked out. For example, Ginny resented the fact that her younger sister Justine got to date at age fourteen, whereas Ginny had had to wait till she turned sixteen. Ginny had proven to her parents that she could be responsible in her midteens; Justine reaped the benefits of her sister's behavior.

Middle children deal with a peer from birth. They contend not only with parental nurturance and authority but also with sibling affection and competition. This is a mixed blessing. On the one hand, middle children start off with a companion, a playmate, a pal. On the other hand, they start off with a rival who almost invariably resents them as newcomers.

Being a middle child brings the consistent advantages of companionship. Similarly, it provides the possibilities of receiving mentorship from older siblings (learning to play and settle differences; having behavior to imitate; getting help with exploring the world) and providing mentorship for younger ones (teaching them to play; modeling behavior; learning to nurture and share).

Depending on where they are in the order of birth, middle children sometimes feel as if they're dealing with not just two parents but three or more. Everyone tells them what to do. Everyone else knows better. They may end up feeling shoved around. Being a middle child is generally less distinguished than being first or last. Middle children may feel lost or overlooked. As Stacey puts it, "I was always being asked, 'Are you Jeff's little sister? Are you Gloria's big sister?' I was always defining who I was by who my brother or sister was. And that has continued to be true ever since."

Finally, depending on the size of the family, being a middle child can mean that other siblings have already staked out the best territory in terms of both physical space (rooms, play areas, and so on) and emotional space (family roles).

Being the last-born child in a family has a reputation for resting in the lap of luxury. To some extent this reputation is deserved. Being the "baby of the family" often means being delighted in, indulged, and favored in ways that older children experienced only temporarily.

Youngest children tend to be seen as creative, playful, extroverted. They often have an outgoing, optimistic view of things. They have a sense of being able to get what they want—and they get a *lot*. Last-born children are frequently indulged by their parents and often by their siblings as well. Families may see them as more helpless and dependent, especially during the earlier years of life; there's a natural tendency for people to take care of them and protect them.

Like middle children, the youngest have several advantages: never having an exclusive parent-child bond to relinquish, finding playmates in place, and having parents who are often less overprotective and anxious than they were with earlier children.

Predictably, there's a flip side to this situation: Last-born children may feel like the low ones on the totem pole. All the other children have staked their claims and acquired their roles; the last-born get whatever's left, which may sometimes prompt them to become re-sourceful. For example, Sarah, her sister, and her two brothers often enjoyed eating M&M's together when they were children. Each child got a certain number of candies; they then traded them and played games with them before indulging in the final feast. But Sarah—the youngest—often held off eating her share till the others had finished. She enjoyed the power this saving gave her: to share her M&M's when the others had none left, to keep them for later, or to eat them while the others watched. Hoarding candy became a way for Sarah to redress the balance of power that so often favored her older siblings.

Finally, the last-born may feel less important than the others pre-cisely because he or she comes last. And older siblings can be resentful of the baby, with uncomfortable consequences for everyone. Brenda recalls the day her oldest sister told her, "You're the reason for all my problems. You got all the attention." In addition, having become accustomed to people taking care of them, youngest children may resist becoming self-sufficient. They experience a strong gravitational pull toward the family. They can suffer from a me-too syndrome as well: Whatever you've got, I want. There's a constant desire to have what the other siblings have, even to be just like them simply because that's what they are.

Another important factor in sibling roles is gender. In most cultures, parents treat boys and girls differently. Modern American culture is no exception. Gender roles—that is, roles assigned according to whether you are male or female—are changing in this country, but distinctions remain in how parents treat their children. Common assumptions are that boys are more aggressive, girls gentler; boys are more physically adept, girls more verbally sophisticated; boys more stubborn, girls more cooperative; and so forth. In some cultures the emphasis goes even further, with a higher premium placed on boys than on girls.

Ultimately, the influence of gender on sibling roles isn't hard to detect. If your parents valued boys more than girls, and if you are female, then their preferences strongly affected how you felt about yourself and your siblings. According to Joanne, "The sun shone where my brother sat." (Or did she mean "The son shone . . ."?) In her parents' eyes, her brother had acquired the place of honor simply by being male. Elaine had a similar experience with her brother—she was the fourth child of parents who had only wanted two kids but "kept on trying," as Elaine put it, "till they got the 'much-awaited son.'"

Similarly, if your parents believed that boys should be aggressive and athletic, and if you—their youngest son—hated sports and preferred intellectual pursuits, their values almost certainly shaped your confidence and self-esteem. If your parents appreciated you for what you were rather than specifically for your being male or female, their open-mindedness surely influenced your development.

*   *   *

Other factors can have a profound influence on your sibling roles. How big was your family? How close in age were you and your siblings? Was one of your parents seriously ill, injured, or handicapped during your childhood? Or did one of your parents die when you were young? Was one of your siblings seriously ill, injured, or handicapped during your childhood? Or did one of your siblings die when you were young? Were you and your siblings raised by someone other than your parents? Were you separated from any of your siblings during childhood? Are your siblings biological brothers and sisters? All these variables can affect your sense of role in your family and, ultimately, in the world.

Family roles are powerful because the family is the first and usually the most intense drama we experience. Family members, more than any other people, have shaped us. Without knowing that they did so, our parents, brothers and sisters, and other relatives cast us in roles that we didn't understand at the time and either accepted or rebelled against. Perhaps we have only now begun to grasp them.

These old roles continue to influence us because the feelings associated with them often end up being reinforced in our interactions with other people. Yet the roles may not be effective; they may no longer be appropriate; they may never have been appropriate. They may inhibit rather than facilitate our growth and change. Like an actor who finds it hard to shed the personality, mannerisms, and behavior of a character in a play, we struggle to be who we want to be.

3

The Cast of Characters

- I was the troublemaker in my family.

- As a kid, I was such a Goody Two-shoes—no wonder I felt a need to be a rebel in my teens.

- My sister was a raving beauty. I could never look half as pretty as she was, so I didn't even try. Instead, I concentrated extra hard on my studies.

- With three brothers who were gifted athletes, I tried to stand out by being more of the artistic type.

Many of us express pride, shame, chagrin, amusement, or exasperation at the roles we acquired or were assigned in our families. Depending on our interests, personalities, and self-confidence (or lack of it), we react with pleasure or displeasure at where we ended up in the family scheme of things. After all, these roles have shaped how we feel about ourselves; they have been among the forces that carried us into adulthood. Yet sometimes our roles end up feeling obsolete. They have ceased to be relevant to who we have become.

There's no question that childhood roles can be a positive influence if harnessed productively during adulthood. For example, Irene was the rebel in her family—a role with highly negative connotations for her parents and siblings, who valued conformity above all else. She felt stigmatized by this label well into young adulthood. As a grown woman, however, she became a lawyer specializing in environmental law and came to value her independent mind and willingness to take controversial stands and confront the "powers that be."

For others, however, childhood roles become restrictive, even suffocating. Mary, for instance, always looked up to her sister Paula as the family "brain." She felt stupid by comparison. Her experiences in school often reinforced this sense of herself. But Mary wasn't stupid—she constrained herself by her expectations of intellectual failure. After attending graduate school for years, Mary dropped out abruptly, reinforcing her self-image as the dummy. Only now has she begun to grasp the fact that anger, rather than stupidity, lies at the heart of her problems. And as she works to identify the sources of her anger, Mary has perceived the possibility of shedding the role of dummy and choosing one that serves her better.

Receiving a label doesn't necessarily make you what that label describes. Danny's family, for instance, tagged him the Lazy Boy from an early age. However, Danny's parents' intense marital problems were prompting them to consider divorce. Danny's "laziness" was most likely a form of depression in response to his family situation. As an adult, Danny is able to recognize that what once prompted others to brand him lazy was an expression of his emotional state; as he better understands the situation, he finds that he has far more energy to undertake the tasks that constitute his life.

Roles are a reality of family life. But they are not cast in stone. What you experience with your siblings contributes to what roles you play in your family. And to some extent your present roles depend not only on your own past roles but also on your siblings' roles, both now and long ago. In effect, your roles are the oars that help you row through family life. Many people feel pressure to maintain their family roles. This pressure is especially forceful in childhood, but it often persists into adulthood. If you can recognize what your roles are, however, in conjunction with what your family's expectations of you have been, you can shed light on what you need to contend with to move beyond these roles.

The heart of the matter isn't the existence of roles but what we do with them. We can choose how we experience ourselves and present ourselves to others. The powerful forces that affected us in childhood may have led us to believe that we can't make choices about our roles. But in fact we can.

What Is Your Role?

Psychologists and other social scientists have devised various schemes for categorizing family roles. The sheer variety and detail of these schemes is less significant for our purposes than the notion that each family tends to tag its members with labels that often shape the roles they acquire. As a psychotherapist, I've observed that many individuals experience a lingering sense of themselves as one "type" or another—a good kid or a troublemaker, someone who is appreciated or someone who is disregarded, and so forth—because of these family labels. Here are the general categories of sibling roles I've noted:

- Whiz Kids
- Wonder Children
- Underachievers
- Do-gooders
- Troublemakers
- Comic Relief
- Heirs Apparent
- Twins
- Miscellaneous

These categories are useful because they provide a kind of "handle" for grasping certain aspects of your identity that you may not have recognized as shaping you. Taking hold of this handle can bring you new insight into how your sibling roles influenced you—and, ideally, how you wish to change them.

The following exercise will help you identify the roles that you used in childhood and may still be using. The checklist indicates characteristics that your family may have attributed to you (or that you may have attributed to yourself) during childhood, during adulthood, or both. Note the characteristics that apply to you by checking the appropriate blank in the relevant column. You may check both blanks for a characteristic if both apply. Choose as many characteristics as apply.

Once you've noted the applicable characteristics, make a list of them by using the codes at the far left of the checklist (e.g., A3, B2, D7, and so forth). The rest of this chapter discusses these characteristics and the family roles that often accompany them. These roles go by many names, of course; the following discussion uses those that seem most common in everyday usage or most helpful in making sense of roles and their effects on us.

	DURING CHILDHOOD	DURING ADULTHOOD	CHARACTERISTICS
			Category A: Whiz Kids
A1	____	____	Unusually bright
A2	____	____	Gifted in the arts, sciences, or some other field
A3	____	____	Academically talented, hardworking, or both
A4	____	____	Acts like a "know-it-all"
			Category B: Wonder Children
B1	____	____	Dazzlingly attractive/beautiful/handsome
B2	____	____	Energetic and ambitious
B3	____	____	Talented in organizing, managing, and encouraging others
B4	____	____	Athletically gifted
			Category C: Underachievers
C1	____	____	Slow to catch on; not that sharp
C2	____	____	Nothing going for him/her; can't seem to make things work
C3	____	____	Physically clumsy, klutzy, careless, accident prone

DURING CHILDHOOD	DURING ADULTHOOD	CHARACTERISTICS
C4	____ ____	Chronically ill, sickly, or injured
C5	____ ____	Low in energy or motivation; everything is an effort
C6	____ ____	Socially withdrawn
C7	____ ____	Complains about everything; whines

Category D: Do-gooders

D1	____ ____	Always helpful, cooperative, obedient
D2	____ ____	Strives to mediate, keep the peace, and resolve conflicts within the family
D3	____ ____	Advises family and friends to help solve their problems
D4	____ ____	Saintly; infinitely helpful and selfless
D5	____ ____	Grudgingly helpful and selfless (often demanding constant recognition for his/her efforts)
D6	____ ____	Helps care for sick/injured family member
D7	____ ____	Responsible for family's physical/financial safety

Category E: Troublemakers

E1	____ ____	Mischievous at home or at school; causes trouble; doesn't live up to standards
E2	____ ____	Makes real trouble, even breaking the law
E3	____ ____	Doesn't "fit in" with others—a loner
E4	____ ____	Resists authority, rebels; does whatever he/she wants
E5	____ ____	Bullies others; overpowers them with strong will and bossy attitudes
E6	____ ____	Tough or "hoody," whether for real or as an act
E7	____ ____	Nonconformist, outrageous, crazy, loony, or flamboyant; may have strange appearance and/or attitudes

Category F: Comic Relief

F1	____ ____	Able to ease tension and conflicts
F2	____ ____	Loves playing jokes/pranks, sometimes at others' expense
F3	____ ____	Always wants to play and party
F4	____ ____	Cheerful, sunny, optimistic; always sees the bright side

Category G: Heirs Apparent

G1	____ ____	Treated as the favorite or special by one or both parents

DURING CHILDHOOD	DURING ADULTHOOD	CHARACTERISTICS
G2	_____ _____	Heroic; always comes through; saves the day
G3	_____ _____	Pseudoparental in role—more like a parent than a brother/sister

Category H: Twins

H1	_____ _____	Seems the same as the other twin
H2	_____ _____	Seems different from the other twin but part of a pair
H3	_____ _____	Negates or disregards the significance of being a twin
H4	_____ _____	Can do no wrong (and is always favored) or can do no right (and never measures up)

Category I: Miscellaneous

I1	_____ _____	Girl with boyish activities or mannerisms
I2	_____ _____	Boy with girlish activities or mannerisms
I3	_____ _____	Always popular and socially involved
I4	_____ _____	Inclined toward solitary pursuits
I5	_____ _____	Socially awkward; nerdy; often academically obsessed
I6	_____ _____	Unattractive (sometimes only as a stage)
I7	_____ _____	Overweight
I8	_____ _____	Emotional, exuberant, lively
I9	_____ _____	Unemotional, subdued

Whiz Kids

Whiz Kids are siblings whose families perceive them as intellectually gifted. The Whiz Kid role is most often seen in a positive light, with special status and privileges; however, in some families a Whiz Kid role may be negative, such as when a child is mocked for being an "egghead."

An example of the Whiz Kid is Jack, the younger of two sons born to highly educated parents. Jack's older brother, Jim, experienced many emotional problems from an early age. Jim did poorly in school and started getting in trouble with the police during his teens. In response to Jim's difficulties, Jack immersed himself in schoolwork and in his study of classical piano. These pursuits mattered to Jack in their own right; however, they also provided a means of distinguishing himself from a troubled sibling in his parents' eyes.

Among the Whiz Kids, the Brain (A1) has uncommon native intelligence of verbal, mathematical, linguistic, or some other sort that shapes the family's perceptions and expectations. This role is based more on potential than on accomplishment.

The Prodigy (A2) is similar to the Brain in having genuine talents (whether intellectual or artistic), but the Prodigy's talents are especially conspicuous for their early appearance. The precocious violinist, dancer, mechanical genius, and painter are all examples of the Prodigy.

By contrast, the Student (A3) is less remarkable for native smarts than for sheer effort, discipline, and persistence. The Student may be bright enough, but he or she stands out mostly by trying harder, studying longer, and taking school more seriously than most other kids.

The Know-it-all (A4) may or may not possess unusual intelligence, artistic gifts, or dedication. He or she doesn't have to. Whether by birth order or by some other status in the family, the Know-it-all simply possesses an overwhelming sense of personal conviction and authority.

Wonder Children

Like Whiz Kids, Wonder Children acquire special status for their native talents; they differ, however, because their gifts are often more a matter of physical appearance or social graces.

Consider Marissa. The youngest of five children, Marissa has been stunningly beautiful at every stage of life. Even complete strangers complimented her parents on her looks when Marissa was a baby; she won the Little Miss Ohio contest at the age of six; she was lovely even during the "awkward stage" of ages eight to eleven; she turned heads and broke hearts from her teens on. Beauty has been as much a fact of Marissa's life as blue eyes or blonde hair. Her two brothers took their youngest sister's appearance more or less in stride; her two sisters, however, resented the constant attention Marissa received. For many years this resentment left Marissa feeling isolated, even stigmatized by her looks—so much so that she "dressed down" to avoid standing out.

Marissa is a classic instance of the Beauty (B1)—the sibling who draws attention chiefly for being pretty or handsome. The Beauty may have other attributes, but attractiveness is what the family has chosen to focus on.

By contrast, the Go-getter (B2) is conspicuous for knowing what he or she wants and for working hard to get it. Go-getters are unusually earnest or driven—real wheeler-dealers—and usually going somewhere in a hurry.

Similar to the Go-getter is the Leader (B3). While the Go-getter has mainly his or her own interests in mind, the Leader is more concerned with the welfare of others. The Leader may be an oldest child—a brother or sister whose age and birth order have led to a sense of authority and responsibility.

Then there's the Athlete (B4). Just as the Student may or may not be intellectually gifted, the Athlete may receive attention either as a consequence of native athletic ability or sheer application. Sports have such a significant role in American culture, however, that even modest accomplishment brings the Athlete considerable attention.

Underachievers

The flip side of the Whiz Kid roles are those we might call Underachievers. Underachievers aren't necessarily "damaged goods"; there may be nothing wrong with them physically or mentally. But they are *perceived,* for whatever reason, to be less capable, less thoughtful, less energetic, less assertive than they ought to be.

Phyllis had always done badly in school, but her influential and well-connected parents managed to get her into a prestigious private academy. Despite her acceptance there, Phyllis always felt embarrassed by her grades. Teachers tried to reassure her: "You're a bright girl—you're just not trying hard enough." But studies were a constant struggle for Phyllis. Her fellow students teased her about her low grades and awkward classroom efforts. Phyllis eventually learned that she is dyslexic, but the damage was done early. She compensated for her poor reading skills by excelling at memorization; still, she always felt tagged the Underachiever. This role haunted her for years. Even as an adult, both at work and in relationships, Phyllis feels unsure of herself and hesitates to assert herself in any way.

Specific kinds of Underachievers include the Dummy (C1), who just can't keep up with his brothers and sisters or peers. Either he's not very bright or he seems that way. Perhaps he suffers from some kind of learning disability; perhaps he's socially inept; perhaps he just doesn't "catch on" as fast as other kids. Or perhaps he's merely an ordinary kid whose family has assigned him this role.

The Loser (C2) may be bright, even brilliant, but just can't accomplish anything. The problem may be emotional conflict, disability, or unrealistic family expectations. As with the Dummy, the Loser may simply have been *tagged.*

The Klutz (C3) is on a collision course with the physical world. The reason varies. Some kids are simply less deft than others. Some are clumsy at certain phases of life, such as adolescence. Some Klutzes aren't naturally klutzy at all—their difficulties are at least partly learned behavior.

By contrast, the Invalid (C4) is the sibling who is either sick or injured, or is perceived to be. In some cases the Invalid has genuine health problems that require a disproportionate share of the parents' time, care, and patience. Sometimes, however, the Invalid isn't sick but has somehow learned to influence family members' behavior with claims of sickness. (Note also that many Invalids aren't underachievers at all—simply children who face more challenges than most.)

The Lazybones (C5) is the child who lives life in slow motion. His "laziness" may be a consequence of health problems, depression, or other causes; some children who seem lazy may be experiencing a physiological or psychological slump, but laziness may also be a learned behavior. In a fast-paced family, for example, one child might reject the customary speed in favor of something more leisurely.

The Wallflower (C6) isn't lazy, just shy. The Wallflower wants to be part of the scene but can't muster the courage to join in. Whether as a stage or as a long-term tendency, the Wallflower has trouble reaching past his or her own shyness.

Finally, there's the Whiner (C7). The Whiner may be perfectly normal, even gifted, but complains so much that he or she wearies everyone around with grumbles, groans, protests, and gripes.

Do-gooders

Some children seem to do no wrong. They are helpful, supportive, and well-intentioned toward both their parents and their siblings. If not always as wonderful as they seem, Do-gooders nonetheless win special approval and affection.

Faye, born two years after her sister Joyce, has felt very different from Joyce for as long as she can remember. Joyce was willful, stubborn, and aggressive; Faye was cooperative and placid. Precisely because her sister seemed to argue so much with her parents, Faye worked hard to please them. She says, "I'm neat and tidy; Joyce is messy. My sister was always late—we'd be ready to go, and she was still not dressed. I hate being messy." Faye wanted so badly to avoid the conflicts that often engulfed her sister that her behavior went beyond mere congeniality. "I also took care of Mom emotionally. I understood her. I kept track of glasses, keys, and her purse. I was the 'fix-it' person at home. I helped out without being asked. My sister did only what she was asked specifically to do and no more. She didn't see things that needed to be done; but I did."

Mommy's (or Daddy's) Little Helper (D1) is the sweetest, kindest, most affectionate, most cooperative child a parent could want. The Little Helper seems too good to be true. Yet these creatures aren't especially rare, and they are often just as helpful, cooperative, kind, and loving as they seem.

The Diplomat (D2) is the child who prevents or eases conflicts between other family members. Some resolve the day-to-day spats that develop among children; others serve as intermediaries between the children and the parents; still others defuse trouble between the parents themselves.

Like the Diplomat, the Counselor (D3) assists family members during times of conflict. Here the emphasis isn't on intervening between members but on giving them advice. The Counselor listens, consoles, makes suggestions, and offers insights. In some cases the Counselor is a kind of in-house family therapist.

While the Diplomat and the Counselor do what is humanly possible for others, the Saint (D4) shoots even higher. Saints have such a strong sense of loyalty and self-denial that they do anything possible to help their parents or siblings. "I'll deny myself and do anything for you" is the Saint's motto.

The Martyr (D5) is the Saint with a grudge. The Martyr, like the Saint, will protect, look after, and help the family but will also remind everyone of these sacrifices every inch of the way. The Martyr resents the very people that he or she insists on helping.

One variation of the Saint is the Nurse (D6), the sibling who looks after everyone's health. The Nurse may have a general duty to keep everyone well, or he or she may have specific responsibilities toward one or more family members (perhaps the Invalid).

Finally, the Protector's (D7) role takes several forms. Sometimes the Protector is a sibling whose age, experience, or size provide a sense of safety to others in the family; at other times the Protector serves as the homemaker when either or both parents are unable or unwilling to do so.

Troublemakers

Another group of siblings can do no right. These are the ones I call the Troublemakers—children who are less cooperative, helpful, or endearing than others in the family or who end up being treated that way. Their negative status may reflect their behavior, but it may result from a comparison with siblings the family perceives in a more favorable light.

Glenn had a troubled life from his early years on. The oldest of three brothers, he was intelligent but suffered from hyperactivity and several learning disabilities. These difficulties prompted Glenn to feel (not entirely without cause) that his parents favored the two younger boys. He expressed his anger and frustration at feeling snubbed by baiting other members of the family, raising hell at school, and shoplifting. Glenn's troubles subsided in his late twenties, when he forged a better sense of himself and established an independent life away from his family.

The Little Devil (E1) is a Troublemaker who annoys others and tests their patience but does no real harm. He or she is more a nuisance than a danger. Unfortunately, the Little Devil role is often self-perpetuating: this label brings with it a degree of notoriety, power, and attention.

The Delinquent (E2) may do genuine harm to others or their property. Delinquents get in trouble at school or with the law; they cause problems at home as well. Sometimes their delinquency is temporary and shallow, sometimes deep-rooted and long lasting.

With the Black Sheep (E3), the issue isn't usually harmful behavior so much as it is inappropriate behavior. What makes a Black Sheep "black" is disregarding the family norms and expectations.

The Rebel (E4) is potentially less destructive than the Little Devil or the Delinquent but shares their resistance to authority. Rebels see themselves as their own bosses. No one can tell them what to do—if someone does, they'll do precisely the opposite.

The Bully (E5) is conspicuous for harassing others. Within the family, the Bully may pick on younger siblings in ways that qualify as genuine abuse or merely obnoxious teasing. This role often suggests emotional problems.

The Hood (E6) cultivates the image of a bad dude without necessarily resorting to genuinely destructive behavior. The Hood just wants to *seem* bad. The Hood is often a teenage role—a channel for expressing contempt toward the older generation and its status quo.

Finally, there's the Crazy One (E7). He or she may or may not *be* crazy; acting crazy is sufficient. Sometimes the Crazy One suffers from real psychological disabilities, but erratic or eccentric behavior may create the same role.

Comic Relief

Another cluster of roles belong to children who provide comic relief in the family drama. These siblings intentionally or unintentionally take a lighter view of life than everyone else and often (though not always) ease the strain of day-to-day tensions.

Morris and Charles are brothers. Tensions between the two were always high during childhood, for Charles felt that their parents favored Morris; Morris, in turn, felt wrongly blamed for Charles's frustrations. For many years, Morris nurtured deep hurt and resentment over his brother's treatment of him. But he gradually discovered that humor eased his tensions and deflected the troubles he encountered. He could often tease Charles out of his bad moods. At school, too, he got out of difficulties by cracking jokes. When a local bully dared him to fight after school one day, Morris pulled out a notebook and said, "Here's my fight schedule—let's see if I can find a slot for you this afternoon. No—sorry, I'm all booked up for fights." This amused the bully enough to defuse the situation.

Among the siblings who provide comic relief, the Clown (F1) is the court jester: joking, horsing around, teasing, making fun of situations that everyone else takes too seriously. The Clown's playfulness serves as a safety valve for the whole family.

By contrast, the Joker (F2) enjoys laughing *at* people more than *with* them. The Joker's jokes have more sting than the Clown's. The Joker may even delight in pranks or tricks in which someone else's shock, fear, bafflement, or humiliation is the punch line.

One variant of the Clown is the Good-Time Charlie (F3). The Good-Time Charlie is concerned less with humor than with general enjoyment of life. What matters to him is hanging out, having a good time, and helping everyone else have a good time as well.

Finally, there's Happy-go-lucky (F4), who sees the silver lining in the darkest cloud. At best, the Happy-go-lucky is a delight to have around: a source of warmth who cheers people up, smoothes over others' misunderstandings, and eases some of the tensions of family life.

Heirs Apparent

I've noted that birth order is a powerful influence on sibling roles. At times a child's "rank" in the family makes such a difference that it's the most obvious feature of the role. Those who receive special attention or accolades from their family—sometimes because of birth order, sometimes because of other factors—are the Heirs Apparent.

Claudia was not only her parents' firstborn but also the firstborn following her mother's long struggle to bear a child. She was the apple of her mother's eye from Day One. As a result, Claudia quickly attained a sense of herself as good, important, competent, and deeply loved. She excelled at every endeavor she undertook. The only drawback was that her younger brother often felt like "second fiddle"; nothing he did seemed to measure up to Claudia's achievements. Claudia loved her brother and regretted his frustrations. As a result, she sometimes strove extra hard—perhaps too hard—to help her brother, to reassure him, to do anything she could to make him feel better. Her brother resented these reassurances as well: They were further evidence of Claudia's remarkable gifts and abilities.

Among the Heirs Apparent, the role of Favorite (G1) isn't determined only by birth order. Which child ends up the Favorite depends on factors such as similarities or differences between the family members' emotional makeup, specific interests, abilities and disabilities, and personality quirks.

The Hero (G2) is a Favorite with an additional cachet. Some families perceive one child as having saved them, or being capable of saving them, from an internal or external threat. Other families bestow the title of Hero on members who merit something less dramatic.

Some families treat the oldest child (often the oldest son) as heroic by default.

If the Hero is a conquering savior, the Pseudoparent (G3) is a foot soldier who puts up a good fight in the day-to-day battle. The Pseudoparent helps the parents (or a single parent) by looking after younger siblings, assisting with domestic duties (cooking, cleaning, shopping), even earning money to support everyone else.

Twins

As I'll discuss in Chapters 12 and 13, twins manifest many of the same issues of sibling rivalry as their nontwin brothers and sisters, yet they have characteristics that are specific to them. For this reason, twins often end up in one of several special roles in the family—many times with particular allegiance to each other.

Bonnie sums up her experience as an identical twin in this manner: "Being a twin probably hampered my having a closer relationship with my other siblings but formed a bond that couldn't be stronger with my twin sister." Duncan, also an identical twin, felt close to both his brothers but had this frustration: "Being one of 'the twins' during high school was irritating. I wanted my own separate identity, and at the time it seemed that I could never be considered an individual."

The Twinny (H1) is a twin the family treats as identical to the other. Predictably, this role is most common when the twins are biologically identical. Families who label their twins in this manner almost always refer to them collectively as "the twins," as if they are a unit rather than two individuals.

By contrast, some twins seem different despite being part of a pair. These twins seem like Tweedledum and Tweedledee (H2)—variations on a theme. Such twins may be either identical or fraternal.

Then there's a role I call the Nontwin Twin (H3): the twin who minimizes or even discounts the significance of being a twin. These twins are often rebelling against the pressure they experience by virtue of their twinship.

Finally, there is the Good Twin/Bad Twin (H4) pair of roles. These roles fit twins who have been categorized in such a way that one appears to be incapable of doing anything wrong and the other appears incapable of doing anything right.

Miscellaneous

My last category is the grab bag: roles that don't fit anywhere else.

The Tomboy (I1) and the Sissy (I2) roles are almost identical in nature but reversed in implication. The Tomboy is a girl who seems boyish or masculine. The Sissy is a boy who seems girlish or feminine. Both roles may reflect family values rather than a child's own nature.

Similarly, the Social Butterfly (I3) and the Loner (I4) are two sides of the same coin. Some children are naturally gregarious; others prefer solitary pursuits. Neither attitude is inherently problematic. Either may suggest a reaction to family attitudes or conditions.

Sometimes the Nerd (I5) is a Brain, Prodigy, or Student obsessed with intellectual pursuits. At other times the Nerd is an Underachiever who can't get organized or motivated. The Nerd may even be just a Wallflower—a shy kid who hasn't blossomed yet. In each case, the Nerd role combines academic inclinations with social isolation.

Two variations on a theme are the Ugly Duckling (I6) and the Fatty (I7). Both are children whose appearance largely determined their roles—in the one case, because of homeliness; in the other, because of obesity. Both the Ugly Duckling and the Fatty roles may be temporary. The original Ugly Duckling in the Hans Christian Andersen tale was, after all, a swan.

A final pair of roles: the Emotional One (I8) and the Quiet One (I9). Families assign these roles on the basis of psychological intensity. Both may have some element of truth. However, both are also relative to what the other children in the family are like.

This exercise provides a thumbnail sketch of you and the different aspects of who you are. It reveals aspects of yourself that you truly like and may want to enhance, as well as aspects that you do not like and may want to change. Seeing all these aspects of yourself more clearly (including their origins—that is, the roles you have accumulated in the context of your siblings and your family) gives you an opportunity to shed old roles and to develop new ones. That is, your new vision of yourself may help you *define* your identity rather than simply *inherit* an identity molded by the past.

Part Two

The Hidden Bonds of Siblinghood

4

The Good-Enough Sibling
and the Supersibling

Roles constitute one of the most important ways we define ourselves as siblings. However, there's another significant aspect of sibling identity: our views of ourselves as "good" brothers or sisters. Are we supportive enough of our siblings? Are we affectionate, distant, or hostile toward them? Are we responsive or unresponsive to their needs? These are some of the questions we constantly ask ourselves in our quest to be good-enough siblings. The answers we hear—which come mostly from observing our behavior toward sisters and brothers—are an important element in shaping how we feel about ourselves.

The Good-Enough Sibling

The core issue most of us struggle with is that of unconditional availability. That is, we think we should be available to our siblings all the time, in all situations, under all circumstances. This expectation is a remnant of the unconditional availability we experienced during infancy. We expected our parents to be there for us always; we came to expect the same from our siblings. Such expectations linger long past childhood, usually with great emotional power. We carry similar high expectations of ourselves well into adulthood: to be unconditionally available to our brothers and sisters.

For these reasons, the idea of putting conditions on our availability to siblings seems alien, unfair, even wrong. Qualifying our willingness to help out may strike us as selfish and stingy, with a consequent lowering of our self-esteem. Never mind that it's physically and emotionally impossible to be available at all times and in all situations; we still expect it of ourselves. Expectations of unconditional availability guide much of our behavior toward siblings.

These expectations and their effects on our behavior give rise to what I call the ideal of the Good-Enough Sibling. From early childhood on, we were all barraged with messages about how we should behave toward our brothers and sisters. Older siblings, for instance, usually hear clear and frequent messages that they should share toys and other belongings with their younger sisters and brothers; they should also protect them, look out for them, be kind to them. Younger siblings hear messages about their own privileges and responsibilities. Bit by bit, each child acquires a set of expectations about what being a good-enough brother or sister entails.

The snag, unfortunately, is that each of us acquires a slightly different set of expectations. Many factors influence us, among them our gender, place in the order of birth, number of siblings, and other individual and family attributes. We end up viewing siblinghood in unique ways. What seems self-evident to your sister may strike you as outrageous. What your brother finds burdensome may appear to you as the very heart of sibling duty. The result is that there's always a discrepancy between *how you see yourself* as a sibling and *how you are seen by family members.* There's a similar discrepancy between how each of your siblings sees himself or herself and how you see each of them. The result is a veritable mine field of expectations and counterexpectations.

Ask anyone to define what it means to be a good brother or sister and you'll tap into his or her interpretation of the Good-Enough Sibling ideal. "Being a good-enough brother means being there in bad times as well as good." "Being a good-enough sister means being emotionally sensitive to my siblings' needs." "Being a good-enough brother means protecting and looking out for my sister." These responses illustrate the expectations that people have about being good enough without knowing *how much* is enough. How often do they have to be there? How sensitive do they have to be? Sensitive to every need? How much do they have to protect? All the time—or just some of the time?

Since all these factors influence expectations, it's not surprising that your concept of the Good-Enough Sibling tends to be abstract and open-ended. You aren't entirely sure what being a Good-Enough Sibling entails, but you expect yourself to live up to the ideal. Yet precisely *because* it is so vague, the ideal of the Good-Enough Sibling complicates the task of recognizing if you have accomplished your goal. As a result, you may often feel guilty despite all you've done for your siblings.

The ideal of the Good-Enough Sibling prompts us to "do the right thing." But assumptions about "the right thing" vary from person to person (depending on personality, family expectations, cultural background) so the ideal itself varies. Each of us has developed an ambiguous and emotionally charged set of assumptions about what makes a sibling good—a standard we then use to evaluate our brothers, our sisters, and even ourselves. We use this standard without much thought, so most of its assumptions remain undefined, unexamined, and sometimes even unnoticed.

Here's an example. Millie's older sister, Janice, often calls Millie to ask for advice and sometimes for financial assistance. For many years, Millie has tried to help Janice through her various crises; at the same time, Millie has struggled with her irritation at Janice's dependence. "She's always calling to talk about her most recent argument with her boyfriend," Millie explains. "Despite my qualms about this man, she insists on going into detail about every aspect of their relationship. I've felt for years that I should be there to hear whatever Janice has to say, but she takes so much of my time that my own relationships are suffering. Things reached a point where I didn't even want to return her calls. I started feeling so guilty. Then Janice would complain that I wasn't giving her enough time. I find her so consuming! She never recognizes my efforts and good intentions. No matter what I give her, she always wants *more*."

Millie's conflict with her sister highlights how this issue involves a disparity between one sibling's expectations and another's. Janice wants an unlimited amount of Millie's time and attention, and demands a certain expression of her loyalty; Millie in turn feels that her sister's demands are excessive. The result is tension. Each feels justified in her position—and both *are* justified, for each feels and sees things differently. The crux of the matter is that each sibling has an ideal of what it means to be a *good-enough* sibling—and each of them has a different definition of this ideal. The challenge to their relationship is to understand better how each defines her idea of the Good-Enough Sibling.

In reality, being a Good-Enough Sibling encompasses behaviors that fall along a continuum. While one person may view being good enough as requiring few actions or emotions, another may view this ideal as involving many specific, rigid obligations. What makes either extreme possible is precisely the lack of a working definition of "good enough." In fact, many of us strive to be good enough precisely by pursuing this ideal without any clear sense of where the pursuit will take us. One result of these far-ranging and often strenuous efforts is overextending ourselves—not being satisfied with being a mere sibling but trying to be some kind of Supersibling (more on this later).

To complicate matters still further, we tend to regard our concept of the Good-Enough Sibling as static. That is, many of us consider the Good-Enough Sibling as a set of attributes—availability, loyalty, patience, warmth, supportiveness, and so on—that never changes. In fact, however, the ideal of the Good-Enough Sibling is often an amorphous mass of ever-shifting expectations, hopes, fears, and obligations rather than a clear, changeless code of sibling honor. Its complexity and tendency to change is in fact what makes the ideal so powerful. Without knowing entirely what our siblings expect of us (and what we expect of them!), we grope toward an expression of being good enough and find it hard to know when we've arrived. The potential for misunderstanding, disappointment, and frustration between siblings is therefore as great as the potential for understanding, satisfaction, and contentment.

The Balance Point

During the 1940s and '50s, the British psychologist D. W. Winnicott defined what he called the "good-enough mother." This concept explains how the focus of a mother's attention on her baby might influence the child for better or worse. The good-enough mother, wrote Winnicott, attends to her infant in terms of the infant's needs rather than her own. An overly attentive mother may ultimately thwart her child precisely by being so attentive. She is *too* good a mother—good to the point that her concerns and attentions prove counterproductive. As the child grows from one developmental stage to another, the good-enough mother continues to realize that her attention must be appropriate to the child's needs.

Bruno Bettelheim, a Viennese-born American psychiatrist, modified Winnicott's concept of the good-enough mother during the late 1980s. Bettelheim called his variation on the theme the "good-enough parent." Part of his concept was acknowledging that both parents affect the child. However, he made another, perhaps even more significant emphasis. "To raise a child well one ought not to try to be a perfect parent," Bettelheim wrote in *The Good Enough Parent,* "much as one should not expect one's child to be, or to become, a perfect individual. Perfection is not within the grasp of ordinary human beings. Efforts to attain it typically interfere with that lenient response to the imperfections of others, including those of one's child." Bettelheim therefore suggested that the goal of parenthood is simply being "good enough." Being a good-enough parent allows the child leeway to develop; in addition, it allows the mother and father a more realistic, less stressful goal for their own task.

The concept of the Good-Enough Sibling derives in some respects from what these theorists have written about parenthood. Both Winnicott and Bettelheim addressed the significance of not giving in excess. While the sibling relationship is, of course, different from the parent-child relationship, there are similarities. Siblings often have a strong emotional bond with one another, as do parents and children. Siblings powerfully affect one another's behavior, as do parents and children.

Just as parents must find a balance between their children's needs and their own, siblings must establish a balance between personal and sibling needs.

How can you attain the ideal of being a Good-Enough Sibling? How can you be a Good-Enough Sibling without endlessly chasing an unreachable goal? How can you honor your siblings without suffering from unrealistic expectations and from the damage those expectations often cause? In short, how can you find the happy medium between too much and too little involvement?

Under the best circumstances, the Good-Enough Sibling is the sister or brother who can be responsive to and caring about siblings' predicaments, problems, and needs in a balanced way—that is, a way that does not negate her or his own needs. The Good-Enough Sibling can *choose* to help rather than *feel obliged* to help. The Good-Enough Sibling is not motivated by guilt, anxiety, intimidation, or fear of siblings' anger. Rather, the Good-Enough Sibling is motivated by his or her choice to "be there." In effect, the Good-Enough Sibling responds to the sister's or brother's needs while leaving room for responsibility to himself or herself.

For example, Anna's sister Hilary is an aspiring actress. At this point in Hilary's career, the parts are few and far between; money is tight, and Hilary often needs financial assistance. Anna feels comfortable helping Hilary financially as a statement of her belief in and support for her sister's artistic endeavors. Anna realizes that she is more financially stable; she wants to share with her sister till Hilary is able to establish herself more securely. Anna doesn't feel coerced or intimidated by Hilary. Her generosity is a choice. For this reason, Anna's help provides a balanced measure of the Good-Enough Sibling, for both Anna and Hilary feel good about their relationship.

By contrast, consider Ted and Dennis. Ever since the brothers were boys, Ted has been Dennis's mentor; Dennis in turn has always looked up to Ted and in some ways has been highly dependent on him. Dennis frequently badgers Ted for advice, guidance, and financial help, though he also regards his brother's loans as a humiliating commentary on his inability to provide for himself. Ted in turn resents his younger brother's constant requests. The brothers are caught in a self-perpetuating cycle of expectations and frustrations—a cycle that neither seems capable of breaking.

Ted and Dennis are at odds mostly because there is a conflict in their ideals of siblinghood. Dennis believes that if Ted were a Good-Enough brother he would continually respond to whatever Dennis needs. Ted is unclear about how much he needs to respond to his brother, so he goes along with Dennis's requests. Thus Ted grows more resentful of his brother without knowing why. Ted needs to define his view of the Good-Enough Sibling—which entails evaluating how much responsibility he can assume for his brother, then setting more realistic limits on the degree of his contribution.

Defining what is truly "good enough" may be difficult and ambiguous, and your sibling may take issue with your definition, yet this process can enrich and heal many sibling relationships.

The Supersibling: Taking the Good-Enough Sibling to Extremes

Do-gooders, discussed in Chapter 3, are the children whose actions many families regard as strongly positive: Mommy's/Daddy's Little Helper, the Diplomat, the Counselor, the Saint, the Martyr, the Nurse, and the Protector. Some boys and girls always seem ready, even eager, to help their parents or siblings, to carry some of the family burdens, to make family life easier and more enjoyable. These siblings may also perform similar functions during adulthood.

Some of these helpful siblings maintain a sense of balance about their roles and duties. However, their helping actions can go awry. Sometimes an individual finds himself or herself with such tremendous responsibility toward one or more sisters or brothers that the role becomes burdensome. The role this sibling acquires is what I call the Supersibling. The Supersibling is the person who feels unconditionally responsible for a sister's or brother's well-being and undertakes all kinds of helping actions to make things better. The Supersibling takes charge and control. If you're the Supersibling, helping isn't an alternative; you feel *you have no choice* but to help your sibling in need. Whatever may be going wrong among your siblings, you feel a vested interest, a responsibility, an obligation to help them.

So what's wrong with wanting to help? After all, these people are your siblings. They're dealing with difficult problems—marital conflict, unemployment, drug or alcohol abuse, physical or mental illness, or any of a great many other major and minor crises. Why not help out? What are families for, anyway?

Certainly there's nothing wrong with wanting to help. Brotherly or sisterly love is one of the best things in life; and there's little doubt that love is a big part of what prompts people to be Supersiblings.

But love isn't the whole story. Other forces also drive Supersiblings to help. Supersiblings, despite their good intentions, often experience severe internal and external pressures—among them guilt, fear, anger, and embarrassment over their sibling commitments. No matter how real your love toward a brother or sister, these pressures can complicate not only your own life but your sibling's as well. In fact, your role as a Supersibling can make things harder—not easier—for everyone involved.

Here are a few stories about actual Supersiblings and their families. These stories do not show the full variety of the Supersibling role; they do, however, provide an initial glimpse of what Supersiblings experience.

When Rita was fifteen years old, a car struck her and severely injured her legs. Recovery took a year of constant care. Some years later, she won a lawsuit filed after her accident and acquired a large amount of money for damages.

The most immediate consequence of this windfall was that Rita became her siblings' financial support system. As she grew older and finished school, Rita found that her sister and brother expected her to support them. Her sister moved into the house Rita had purchased for herself. If someone needed money, Rita provided it. She bought her brother a car. She obtained health care for her sister when her sister had a baby. Rita ended up looking after her siblings without knowing how this arrangement had developed.

*   *   *

Steven was finally on the right track after a tough year spent straightening out his life. He was feeling good about himself and doing well at work—so well, in fact, that the company offered him a better job in another state. He jumped at the chance and made plans to move out of the family's house for the first time.

Then came the phone call. A local emergency room informed him that his older sister had suffered an emotional breakdown and would soon be admitted to the psychiatric unit. Steven felt he had no choice but to drop everything and stick around.

Steven's mother had died long ago; his father had remarried and seemed disengaged from his children ever since. Steven ended up carrying a nearly parental burden for his sister. His daily life now sank under an avalanche of hospital paperwork and family conflicts. Worse yet, the crisis created great emotional upheaval, since one of Steven's brothers is also mentally ill. Perhaps the worst aspect of all was Steven's fear that he wasn't exempt. If his brother and sister were mentally ill, could he suffer the same fate?

Steven began to feel defeated and hopeless. No matter how hard he tried, he believed that he couldn't break free from his siblings' problems.

When Gary was eight, his mother asked him to watch over Judy, Gary's six-year-old sister. This was not an unusual arrangement; Gary often looked after Judy. To make matters worse, the girl was hyperactive—a real handful. That day, while the two children played, Judy fell off a curb and struck her head. Gary's mother returned home at just about that time. Irate, she told Gary, "This accident is all your fault!" and she added that if his sister had any problems resulting from it, she would blame Gary for them as well. She added, "You'd better watch out for her from now on."

Gary took that warning to heart. Throughout childhood, adolescence, and adulthood, he focused his attention more on his sister than on himself. He took on many of Judy's responsibilities—at home, at school, in the outside world. There was little he wouldn't do to help his sister.

As it turned out, Judy had plenty of problems. Early conflicts in school and at work were the least of them. Her drug addiction disrupted the whole family for years. All along, Gary has attempted to prop up his sister by giving her money, offering constant emotional support, and serving as mediator between Judy and the rest of the family. And from childhood till the present Gary has struggled with intense feelings of guilt that somehow—despite all he's doing—he ought to be doing more.

These stories suggest some aspects typical of Supersiblings. The most common of these aspects are genuine love and concern for siblings; a demanding brother or sister who is struggling with personal problems; a sense of heavy responsibility for solving those problems, often at the expense of the Supersibling's own personal or family activities; a feeling that there is no choice but to shoulder that responsibility and its attendant burdens; guilt, resentment, anger, confusion, and helplessness resulting from the contradictions that these circumstances create.

This tangle of issues is not inevitable. It is possible to be a good-enough brother or sister without taking on the Supersibling role. Many people find, in fact, that they are more helpful once they learn to choose how and when to assist their brother or sister rather than feeling unconditionally obliged to help. It is possible to become a Good-Enough Sibling rather than a Supersibling.

Why do some brothers and sisters take on the Supersibling role? As with most roles, some form of external influence has made a difference. Sometimes one of the parents has died, leaving a surviving son or daughter to assume (or be forced into) a quasi-parental role. In other instances, the mother's or father's illness created an expectation that one child in the family would take on special responsibilities. A physically present but emotionally distant parent or a dysfunctional parent (one who is alcoholic, drug dependent, mentally ill, or impaired in some other way) often creates the same sort of situation. In each case at least one child ends up shouldering a disproportionate and often inappropriate degree of responsibility. Sometimes this burden exceeds that carried by the parent or parents.

However, some people become Supersiblings as a consequence of far less drastic events. Birth order can create the Supersibling role. The father of twelve children once expressed the situation in these terms: "In a family as big as ours, you can't be a parent to each kid all the time. You have to run your family like an army. My wife and I are the generals. The older kids are the colonels and captains. The younger ones are the sergeants, lieutenants, and privates. We give the orders, and the orders go down the line." This family's military structure, though perhaps understandable, may place unusual stresses on the children, each in a different way, with both the older and the younger siblings given their own respective sets of "marching orders." For one or more siblings, these "orders" may be experienced as an assignment of the Supersibling role.

Culture also makes a difference. Many ethnic groups have special expectations for the female children's contributions to family welfare. Girls often help with domestic tasks to a degree far beyond anything demanded of boys. The same holds true for child care. Under such conditions it is easy for girls and young women to end up assuming a sense of responsibility toward their siblings—not only the responsibility they were assigned but also what they consciously or unconsciously assume. Similarly, some cultures place high expectations on family loyalty for both men and women, including assumptions that one or more siblings will carry a disproportionate burden looking after the others.

Some people become Supersiblings only upon reaching adulthood. As brothers and sisters grow older, their sense of family loyalty often becomes more pronounced. In relatively healthy families, the sibling bond itself exerts a strong pull. In disrupted families, however, the only linkage people have may be to their sisters and brothers. Meanwhile, parents age; they experience difficulties with their health, mobility, or financial resources; they inadvertently or intentionally increase the pressure on their grown children to take more responsibility for family decisions as a consequence of guilt or ambivalence.

In all these situations, family structure combines with personal circumstances to place a sister or brother in the role of Supersibling. The specific circumstances differ greatly; the results, however, share many features. As often as not, the Supersibling takes on a disproportionate and potentially burdensome degree of responsibility.

Inherent within the Supersibling role is the Good-Enough Sibling quest. That is, anyone who is a Supersibling is struggling to attain the ideal of the Good-Enough Sibling. Supersiblings simply take it to the extreme. They feel a limitless obligation to be the best, the kindest, the most patient, the most creative, the most nurturant brother or sister imaginable. Only by doing so will they meet their expectations for being the Good-Enough Sibling.

How should you work to disengage from the expectations and obligations of being a Supersibling and move to a more realistic working definition of being a Good-Enough Sibling? How can you avoid being held hostage by an ideal whose emotional "cost" is too high for anyone to pay? And how should you deal with the demands that needy siblings with troubles may be making on you?

5
Coping with Supersibling Issues

The Supersibling feels an obligation to go "above and beyond the call of duty" in attending to brothers' and sisters' needs. This obligation derives from a variety of family influences, but what often hooks a Supersibling is a sister's or brother's emotional turmoil. In such situations, the Supersibling experiences an intense need to help.

For example, Noreen, the younger of two sisters, was less favored than her sister. Barbara, the older child, knew a lot about getting her kid sister to do what she wanted. Whenever Noreen complained that Barbara was taking her toys or hitting her, their parents would scold Noreen for whining. "Work it out yourselves," their mother would tell them. Noreen soon grew accustomed to letting Barbara push her around.

The real turmoil, however, began during the sisters' adolescence. When she was a teenager, Barbara was in a car accident and suffered severe injuries. She recovered from her injuries, but the period of her recovery gave rise to difficulties that plagued the sisters for years. Their parents were rightly protective of Barbara during the early months of her convalescence; later, though, they sheltered Barbara so completely that their protectiveness backfired. Among other things, their parents expected Noreen to look after her sister almost like a baby-sitter. Noreen felt burdened by this role, and the situation worsened the girls' attitudes toward each other.

Noreen ended up feeling that, if she didn't take care of her sister, her parents would hold it against her. In response to these expectations, Noreen assumed as much of the parental role as her mother and father did. Noreen should not, in fact, have taken over such extensive duties. If their parents felt that Barbara's activities needed restrictions, they should have put some in place themselves.

Noreen's duties in the family continued for several years. Even when Noreen got married, her obligations toward Barbara did not diminish. She could never quite shake the feeling that she should look after her sister. Barbara still heavily depends on her for help and guidance, and Noreen still feels a need to provide it. Barbara calls Noreen whenever she's in a predicament, which is often; she asks for loans and advice; she berates Noreen when the help she offers doesn't solve all Barbara's problems.

Noreen isn't sure what to do. She resents her sister's weight on her shoulders but worries about Barbara and wants to help her cope with her many difficulties. Noreen feels a great sense of duty to Barbara, yet she isn't quite sure what that duty entails or where her obligations leave off and Barbara's duties toward herself begin.

Noreen is a classic Supersibling. She manifests all the signs outlined in Chapter 4: genuine love and concern for siblings; a demanding brother or sister who's struggling with personal problems; a sense of heavy responsibility for solving those problems; a feeling that there's no choice but to shoulder that responsibility and its attendant burdens; and strong negative feelings that result from these difficult circumstances. In addition, Noreen's situation and her perceptions of it prompt her to feel that she's trapped. She simply has no choice but to solve all problems, ease all worries, lift all burdens, boost all egos, heal all wounds.

Whereas Noreen's instance is clear-cut, you can also fall into the Supersibling role when dealing with siblings who are not so deeply troubled—siblings whose garden-variety problems place demands on you all the same. You may feel your siblings' constant pressures to telephone, to baby-sit, to be compassionate. Being a Supersibling isn't always a response to dire straits; it is also a response to an array of obligations experienced whether there is a great need or not. Sometimes you may wind up as a Supersibling out of concern for a sibling's ongoing, low-grade problems.

For instance, Wendy is the oldest of six siblings. At an early age she acquired the role of Mommy's Little Helper, and she gained attention and praise in this role. However, it has carried over in ways that seem out of proportion. Even as a young adult, Wendy lives at home and takes care of her younger sisters and brothers. If one of her sisters finds her schoolwork difficult, Wendy meets with the teachers. If one of her brothers gets into trouble, Wendy feels a need to intercede.

Denise presents another example of low-grade family problems that result in a Supersibling role. Denise always felt a great need to get along with her siblings—a situation that left her vulnerable. Her older sister, Meredith, made especially great demands on Denise, in terms of both time and money. Denise went along with her sister's expectations. Her "duties" included helping Meredith look after her two children, clean her house, and do some of her shopping. Denise also lent Meredith money when her finances got tight. Even while Denise struggled as a single parent to raise her own child, Meredith expected all sorts of help. Denise explains her situation with a shrug: "Meredith is in a fix these days—I don't know how she'd manage without me."

How Siblings Snare, Hook, and Trap You

Many people feel frustrated by their siblings' responses to their heartfelt and strenuous efforts to help. They knock themselves out to provide assistance but end up feeling unappreciated, even criticized, for not doing enough or for doing the wrong thing. How can siblings be so ungrateful?

There are several reasons for these responses, not least that many brothers and sisters are so caught up in their own needs that they have little or no awareness of anyone else's. Their problems simply exert too great a pull on their attention to allow concern for others. In addition, however, certain emotional problems may actually prompt your sibling to berate or criticize you specifically to increase your efforts to help. This is especially common in families where one sister or brother has assumed the Supersibling role: The Supersibling is, after all, the one "assigned" to help any other family member in trouble. And the Supersibling himself or herself may be a willing accomplice in this state of affairs.

So how should you deal with this situation? One of the best things you can do is to gain some perspective on what's happening. Part of this perspective comes from understanding the issues we've already discussed: your role, its origins, the emotions associated with it, and the steps you can follow to take hold of the situation. In addition, however, you can help yourself by understanding that there are several kinds of siblings whose behavior can snare you in particular ways. This insight can be a useful lens for clarifying the way you react to your brother or sister.

The Rejecting Sibling demands attention and help but puts up road-blocks or obstacles to whatever suggestions or assistance you offer. Basically, Rejecting Siblings just want to vent their frustrations. If you don't allow Rejecting Siblings to do this, they may have to do something about their problems—precisely what their behavior strives to avoid. At times, if the help isn't just what they want, Rejecting Siblings won't accept any help at all. When Rejecting Siblings behave like this, what can you do but try harder? Sharon, for instance, was going to move from one apartment to another. Her brother Ken offered his help but was available only on the morning of the move. Sharon was indignant at her brother's timing: Ken wouldn't come over that afternoon, which was when Sharon wanted his help, so she told him not to bother coming at all. Whatever the nature of your help, the Rejecting Sibling will find fault with it.

The Starving Sibling seems insatiable in his needs for support, money, affection, time, and energy. After Joan's daughter got sick, her sister Peggy spent almost unlimited time helping to care for the girl. Eventually, however, Peggy needed some time out. Joan was furious. How could she take time off when Joan's need was so great? No matter how much time Peggy gave, it wasn't enough. Faced with someone who's so desperately hungry, what can you do but try to feed her more?

The Entitled Sibling feels that others owe her all their best efforts. In her company, what can you do but continue giving in the hope of her acknowledging you? Susan asked her brother Paul for a loan of five hundred dollars. Paul refused, explaining that he didn't have the money. Susan then got angry at her brother, and she accused him of not really caring about her. "You should be glad I'm only asking you for five hundred dollars," she said. "I could have asked for a thousand."

The Martyred Sibling accepts help as if it's a burden for *him* to carry and he is doing *you* a favor. When the Martyred Sibling is so clearly wounded by the world's slights, what can you do but make your help even easier to accept? Jason had been having stomach pains for months. His brother, Alex, at first hinted that he should see a doctor; then he suggested it outright; then—as Jason's complaints increased in number and intensity—Alex badgered him to go. Still, Jason refused. "How about if I drive you there?" Alex asked him. Finally, Jason relented, saying, "All right, all right—I'll go! Your nagging is too much for me to deal with."

The Retaliating Sibling not only resents what others do (or don't do) but explicitly or implicitly threatens to get back at them for not doing enough. If you're in so much danger from this sibling's retaliation, what can you do but keep on trying to appease her? Nathan asked his brother Matthew for a loan. Matthew refused the request. Nathan then borrowed Matthew's car, which Matthew worried Nathan would wreck. When Nathan returned the car unharmed, he told his brother that he should be glad it was all in one piece. One way or another, the retaliating sibling makes you pay.

These kinds of siblings keep you engaged with their problems. They nudge, wheedle, cajole, bribe, threaten, and blackmail you into staying committed to helping them.

Three aspects of these siblings and their ploys deserve further mention:

First, a sibling may or may not use just one ploy to keep you wrapped up in his or her problems. Some of the most troubled brothers and sisters may employ a whole arsenal of techniques to keep you fully mobilized on their behalf.

Second, the phenomena described here aren't exclusively experienced by people in the Supersibling role. You may find yourself pulled into a situation simply as a sibling who's uncertain about your responsibilities to your sister or brother. That is, you risk being manipulated by siblings' behavior whenever you are unclear about the boundaries of your Good-Enough Sibling ideal.

Third, each of these kinds of manipulative sibling behavior requires you to set limits. In fact, without some sort of thoughtful, organized response to difficult siblings, you may find yourself pulled deeper and deeper into their counterproductive attitudes and behaviors.

Coping with Feelings

Dustin and his sister Kira had always been close growing up. As adults, however, their relationship was something Dustin had never expected. The first sign of trouble came when Kira called to tell Dustin that she'd just lost her job. Could she stay with Dustin for a while? Dustin had just gotten married and didn't want a visitor, but Kira showed up anyway and settled in for almost a month. The visit seemed endless. Kira was impatient and demanding. She treated Dustin and his bride as if they were the incompetent managers of a country inn rather than her brother and sister-in-law. She came and went abruptly, never informing them of when she would be back or whether they could expect her for meals. Sometimes she disappeared into the guest room, locked the door, and hid for hours at a time.

Not long after that difficult visit, Kira got a new job, but she lost it almost at once. Dustin offered to help Kira out financially but received only criticism for his help. Dustin soon began to recall other instances when Kira had had trouble at work or when her behavior had seemed erratic or abusive. Before long Dustin suspected that Kira's problem wasn't just unemployment but alcoholism. Even so, he didn't know how to deal with his sister. He was angry about how Kira treated him, but he felt a dizzying mix of other emotions as well: embarrassment at having an alcoholic sister, guilt at not being able to ease her burdens, fear about what would become of her, and ambivalence about the sheer variety and complexity of these feelings.

Dustin's situation is surprisingly common. One of the reasons that Supersiblings often experience such difficulties is that they have become entangled in a web of emotions allowing little or no room for movement. Caught in this web, Supersiblings struggle with an array of feelings without even knowing what they are, much less what to do about them. As one of my patients put it, "How can I deal with my feelings when I don't even know what it is I'm feeling?"

For this reason, the first step toward solving this dilemma is to find yourself ("find" in the sense of discovering your feelings) in this emotional web. And the way to find yourself is to define your feelings—that is, to develop an awareness of what you are experiencing emotionally.

The first step toward developing emotional awareness is to recognize your emotional styles. By "styles" I mean what you do with your feelings. Some people deal with their feelings by minimizing them—pretending that nothing important is happening. If you're angry at your sister for her demands on you, for instance, you may try to dismiss your anger by saying, "Oh, it's no big deal—nothing to get upset about." Some people ignore their feelings altogether, as if nothing has happened. Others externalize the situation, saying, "If I weren't having so much pressure at work, these family problems wouldn't be getting me down." Each of these responses suggests a different emotional style. Other indicators of your state of mind include behaviors such as uncharacteristic forgetfulness, overeating, clumsiness, or consumption of alcohol—anything that suggests a level of stress or emotional upheaval that you're not acknowledging.

Let's say you've had a major argument with your brother. The same evening, in the middle of an otherwise ordinary discussion with your husband, you end up yelling at him. You may be tempted to see the two incidents as separate, but they probably aren't. Under the circumstances, you would do well to trace the connections between these two powerful emotional outbursts. Otherwise, your feelings are going to keep erupting unpredictably.

Once you've taken stock of your feelings, what's next? In the preceding instance, you can finish up the frustrating conversation with your brother, and, instead of lashing out at your husband, you can decide how to change your interactions with a sibling whose actions and statements are troubling you. In other situations, you can take a more specific reading of your emotions and take concrete steps to regain control of what's happening.

I'm suggesting that part of relinquishing the Supersibling role is dealing with intense and unmanageable emotions by first becoming able to distinguish particular feelings from one undifferentiated mass.

The following are the most significant feelings that make life stressful for Supersiblings.

Guilt

If you are a Supersibling, guilt is probably one of the most difficult emotions you're feeling. The reason is that guilt often keeps you stuck in your role. It's what keeps you rooted in the sense of obligation to give and to keep giving—regardless of whether your efforts are what your siblings need or want. Understanding guilt is therefore one of the most crucial tasks facing you.

Guilt creates a powerful and usually destructive catch-22. To direct adequate time and energy toward your own interests and responsibilities, you must limit the time and energy you direct toward your sister's difficulties. Making your own life satisfying means redirecting physical, emotional, and even financial resources from your sister to yourself. So far so good. But here's the catch. The more you say yes to yourself, the more you'll be successful and happy in your own right. In itself, that's no problem. But then you're likely to feel guilty. Your decisions will give you a sense of more satisfaction in life, while your sister still has less than you do—or at least it seems that way. And your sister may well resent you more as a consequence. You'll then feel guilty for keeping time, energy, and other resources to yourself, thus leading you to a renewed sense of obligation to your troubled sister. This cycle of disengagement and guilt, guilt and reengagement, more disengagement and more guilt, can go around indefinitely.

What's the solution? You may have to back off from your sister, then deal with the guilt that comes from becoming separate and successful; you may, in short, have to learn to accept your success on its own terms, *without equating your success with making your sister "get better."*

Don't complicate your situation by letting guilt prompt you to ignore your own needs. Accept feeling guilty without feeling the need to do something that would make the guilt go away. For example, one of my patients had been helped by her sister some years earlier; now the sister made demands on my patient, prompting her to feel an obligation to reciprocate. My patient felt guilty because she found her sister's demands excessive to the point of extortion. In fact, troubled siblings often use guilt as a hook to pull their brothers and sisters closer: "It's your fault that I'm this way." They *want* you to feel guilty. At such times, you should ask yourself why (if at all) you are to blame. More times than not, you aren't. You may still end up feeling guilty—but the emotion of guilt doesn't in any way mean that you are at fault.

"I should help her because she's my sister." I've heard this rationale countless times. That's the sibling bond talking—a powerful voice. Admittedly, it's worth hearing, but is it worth obeying? Not always. When your conscience seems to tell you to help out simply from sibling obligation, you should evaluate the situation more closely. Begin by looking at what you expect of yourself as a Good-Enough Sibling. Are these expectations realistic?

The following five techniques for dealing with guilt can be helpful. As a starting point, I recommend this sequence of steps:

First, *identify the source and the nature of your guilt.* Ask yourself where the guilt came from and what it is about. For instance, if your sister requested financial help and you refused to provide it, you might say, "I feel guilty because I should have given her the money." Are you feeling guilty because you should have done something to help your sister (even if it wasn't to give her money) but you didn't? Or is it because you used the money she wanted on yourself instead? Sometimes you can find other ways to help your sibling; for instance, you might spend more time with her.

Second, *evaluate your expectations as a brother or sister.* That is, define what you expect of yourself as a Good-Enough Sibling. What does your Good-Enough Sibling ideal consist of? You can use the dilemmas that arise with your siblings to develop a practical definition of the Good-Enough Sibling for yourself. This entails a realistic appraisal of how available you can be. Don't expect to get it all right from the start. Use each situation to learn for the next time.

Third, *change your expectations* to be more appropriate to the actual situation. Is giving her money a real solution to your sister's problems? Perhaps so; probably not. If her difficulties involve drug addiction, alcoholism, gambling, or any number of other problems, then a loan not only helps her postpone facing reality but perpetuates her problem as well. In such a case your goal should be changing your own inappropriate expectations that money will help your sister as much as you hope it will.

Fourth, *learn to see what happened as part of a process.* You may or may not have acted wisely in the situation that now makes you feel guilty. After all, you're human; you're capable of making mistakes. Give yourself the leeway to learn from experience. If you really should have loaned your sister money, you'll know better in the future; you can respond differently next time. If, however, some aspect of the request wasn't realistic, then you may have acted wisely in the first place.

Finally, the most important tactic for dealing with guilt is simply to *know that it will pass without your having to do something about it.* It's all right to feel guilty; guilt is part of being human. Simply waiting will often make a big difference. Waiting is admittedly a sizable task. But if you can learn to tolerate the discomfort that accompanies your self-growth, you can build emotional "muscle" that helps you withstand the guilt.

These techniques drive at redefining your personal criteria for being a good-enough sister or a good-enough brother. Perfection really isn't attainable, so try simply to be good enough.

Anger

Almost everyone finds anger difficult to handle. We get angry at our siblings for any of a thousand things: making us feel inept as brothers and sisters, frustrating us in our efforts to help them, needing our help in the first place, evoking our guilt. Many sources of anger toward siblings involve day-to-day misunderstandings and frictions. Others are more intense, the result of siblings' efforts to manipulate, aggravate, or lash out for real or imagined offenses.

All too often, we wind up angry because we give unconditionally and end up feeling lost as a result—feeling unimportant and unappreciated in our siblings' eyes. Even when we want to limit our actions, we continue to overdo. The result is often anger toward our siblings.

You must now start to see things differently: looking through your own eyes rather than through those of your siblings. Don't let your emotions blind you; maintain your clarity of vision. For if you give constantly and without any conditions to your siblings, you're going to churn up a lot of resentment. It's okay to give to your sister, but watch out for losing track of yourself in the process.

Something else to understand about anger is that feeling angry doesn't always mean you must directly express what you feel to the person you're angry with. What is most important is identifying that you're angry and staying in touch with the way you feel. Once you have recognized and accepted your anger, you can determine what will best resolve the situation. Do you hope to change your relationship with your sibling? If so, it will be important for you to express your anger directly so that your brother or sister can know how you feel. Alternatively, can you accept your sibling's limitations and the limitations in your relationship? If so, you can use your anger to help define new boundaries for yourself so you don't continue to feel so overextended. As you begin to do more for yourself, you will feel less irate.

As with guilt, several steps can help in managing anger. Here are three specific recommendations:

First, *identify what you feel angry about.* Clarify the sources of your anger in the most specific terms possible. Rather than saying, "I'm angry at my sister," zero in on her particular actions or attitudes. The statement "I'm angry at her because she's emotionally troubled and hard to deal with" takes things a step further. You might go still further, pinpointing the exact situations, statements, or deeds that infuriate you. "I'm angry because she doesn't have a job and yet expects me to help her out financially."

Second, *define how this situation makes you feel about yourself.* Look at how your anger at your sibling makes you feel toward yourself. Are you feeling that you're not a Good-Enough Sibling? Are you floundering as a Supersibling? Are you angry because you feel inept, stuck, burdened, or helpless? Do you have a sense of loss? What leaves you feeling so negative? Are you angry at your sister because she attacked all your efforts to show you care? Ultimately, your self-esteem as a Good-Enough Sibling is being challenged, so try to recognize in what ways the challenge is occurring.

Finally, *determine what you can do to strengthen your view of yourself as a Good-Enough Sibling.* You can't change what your sibling does or thinks. You can, however, change your attitude so that your sibling's behavior ceases to affect you. What can you change in *yourself* rather than trying to change your brother or sister? Where can you comfortably help? Where can you set some limits? Some of the techniques that work in dealing with guilt are also effective with anger—especially trying to be "good enough" rather than perfect.

Fear

In dealing with a troubled sibling, many adults feel not only guilty and angry but also frightened. They find themselves living in an atmosphere of fear. Some of this fear is for the sibling's health, safety, and sanity—perhaps even for his or her life. But there are other sources of fear as well. One common fear is that of more burdens: having to take on yet further responsibility; having to accept greater financial obligation; having to deal with more crises. Many people fear for the stability—even the survival—of family relationships. And they fear their family's disapproval. Most of all, people are afraid of a brother's or sister's anger.

For instance, Robin's brother Bruce asked to move in with her while he got his life in order. Robin didn't want to share her house but feared that, if she refused his request, Bruce would stop helping her with domestic projects and repairs. When I asked Robin how much Bruce really did for her, however, she admitted that he rarely followed through on his offers to help out. His role as handyman was more illusion than reality. Yet Robin feared that, if she confronted him, she would lose even this comforting illusion. Moreover, she would have to deal with Bruce's anger.

If you feel this sort of fear, what probably underlies it is a feeling that if you were to cease being there at all times in all ways—in short, if you were to cease being Superbrother or Supersister—your sibling would collapse, go crazy, or flee forever. If you were to cease being the Supersibling, everyone would explode in a flash of resentment and disappear.

Such fears are very common. After all, people in a family want each member to play his or her own role. If you're a Supersibling, your role has been that of the Helper, the Diplomat, the Counselor, the Protector. Is it any surprise that everyone else in your family wants the Helper to keep helping? Given the propaganda and pressure that Supersiblings experience, it's predictable that you fear losing your place in the family if you don't play the part you've been assigned.

However, most people find that when they cut free from the Supersibling role, not only do they not lose but they gain. Many are surprised by this turn of events. Yet is it really so surprising? After all, the change of role—the end of excessive helping—almost always means that the Supersibling treats himself or herself with more respect.

This newfound self-respect can only make the person stronger. Other people (sometimes even the siblings!) ultimately notice this strength. Also, many siblings are hungry enough that even though they'll still grumble, they will take whatever support and attention they can get. This is especially true of the Starving Sibling and the Rejecting Sibling. You need to understand that some siblings will be dissatisfied *no matter what you give them.* This realization gives you some freedom to follow your own sense of what's appropriate rather than using your sibling's complaints as the guiding principle. In addition, while some grumble, others lay on so much appreciation and gratitude that they hook you for life.

You may discover that, as you gain in self-respect, you find the security to think more clearly and to act more confidently. By becoming stronger and less driven in your need to help, you haven't lost a thing. You have only gained. And ultimately your new strength provides you with the means to offer your siblings more support rather than less.

Embarrassment, Deprivation, Emptiness

Three other related emotions come out of conflicted sibling relationships—emotions that are essentially by-products of having a troubled sibling. Although intertwined, each of these emotions is different in both its origins and its effects. Realizing that you experience these feelings and understanding their origins can be helpful in coping with them.

Embarrassment usually stems from the social stigma of having a sibling who is seriously troubled, either physically or emotionally. Even the most broad-minded, compassionate people often feel at least some degree of embarrassment over their siblings' difficulties. You can feel embarrassed when out with your brother socially because of his appearance or behavior. You may feel embarrassed talking about your sister when people ask about her and how things are going. People often feel uncomfortable because they believe they'll be measured in terms of their siblings' limitations.

Deprivation comes from the feeling of not having a healthy, enjoyable sibling relationship, not being able to take part in your sibling's life by spending time together or sharing the events of marriage and parenthood. You may feel deprived of a feeling of family and of the closeness and intimacy you want with your sisters and brothers. Deprivation comes from knowing that you won't share the positive aspects of being a brother or sister that you long for; you will experience more of the negative aspects. Responding to the imbalance, you feel deprived of the good feelings that other siblings share.

Emptiness follows in turn. Lacking the experiences you wish to share with a sibling, you feel empty. There is little or no chance for attaining whatever aspects of a brotherly/sisterly relationship you crave but find absent, such as extended family relationships including in-laws and nieces and nephews. You must therefore reconcile yourself to reality and round out your life by other means.

Embarrassment, deprivation, and emptiness often combine to create physical fatigue. The tasks of helping a difficult brother or sister can leave even the most energetic, competent adults feeling drained. Many Supersiblings describe themselves as feeling "out of gas" or "running on empty." In short, these emotions can have physical effects.

How should you deal with these feelings? As with guilt, anger, and fear, the first step is to determine more specifically what you are feeling embarrassed, deprived, or empty *about*. You can then begin to look to other people and experiences to find some nourishment and support for yourself. For instance, though Chloe lacks a close relationship with her sister, she has found a terrific best friend. She can find emotional sustenance with this friend during holidays and on special occasions.

Ambivalence

The final emotion we should consider isn't really a single emotion but a mix—sometimes a jumble—of several emotions. This is ambivalence. What makes ambivalence especially difficult is that the emotions you feel are often exact opposites of each other. You love your brother but hate him. You feel compassion for your sister but feel contempt as well. You feel nurturant toward your siblings but simultaneously desire to reject them.

To complicate matters, our culture places a strong emphasis on feeling "pure" emotions. Love, for instance, should be undiluted by selfishness, envy, fatigue, or impatience—much less polluted by anger and hate. How can you love your brother and hate him at the same time? Ambivalence (especially when it's intense) prompts us to question our motives and values.

In fact, ambivalence is very much a human emotion. Few feelings exist in a pure state. But it's hard to tolerate feeling ambivalent toward our sisters and brothers; the internal stress is intense. This is all the more difficult because ambivalence rarely has a resolution. We may struggle to feel one way or the other—"I should either hate him or love him, but not both"—yet usually we find that both emotions, or several, or many, persist.

The task with ambivalence therefore is to let emotions coexist within you. This is easier said than done; still, it's possible. By accepting yourself as someone capable of feeling many emotions (and sometimes all at once), you can start to move from an ideal notion of siblinghood to something more practical. Don't hold on to the hurts of siblinghood. Accept the fact that you love your sisters or brothers and that they will nonetheless disappoint you, hurt you, even enrage you at times. Ambivalence is not failure. On the contrary, our capacity to feel many feelings at once, and to tolerate the diversity of emotion within us, is part of what ultimately makes our relationship diverse, rich, and powerful.

Becoming a Good-Enough Sibling

Now the rub—the real stickler. In light of all the issues we've discussed so far, how much responsibility toward your sibling is realistic, fair, and right?

Admittedly, determining this degree of responsibility is the hardest task in becoming a Good-Enough Sibling. There is no simple, universal answer. To make matters worse, your family will probably be ready to tell you what to do. (As if you haven't noticed, families are notoriously eager to specify just how other family members should live their lives.)

In fact, degree of responsibility is an individual choice. Acknowledging it as *your own choice* is itself a major step. Making the determination without influence from sisters, brothers, and parents is an act of considerable courage and personal clarity of mind.

There are times, of course, when you face the choice of doing more than is personally comfortable. How should you proceed?

Here's an example:

Molly's sister, Tess, asked Molly to come out for a visit. Tess had been feeling overwhelmed by her professional and parental responsibilities, and she wanted her sister's company. Molly, however, had recently changed jobs and was also breaking up with her boyfriend; she felt too emotionally depleted to travel. Despite Tess's genuine needs, Molly was consumed by the demands of her own life. Molly wasn't sure what to do. She wanted to be a Good-Enough Sibling and be there for her sister, but she also wanted to take care of herself and stay home.

The crux of this kind of situation is *to determine what you feel you can comfortably do.* "Comfortably" does not mean in a carefree, selfish manner. Rather, it means doing what does justice to your overall sense of what seems appropriate. Molly's task was to find the balance point of *her* sense of comfort. After considering her options, she resolved to visit Tess but to limit the length of her stay. This allowed her to provide her sister with some emotional support without greatly depleting her own already low reserves. If Tess is always asking Molly to visit, and if Molly is always putting her own needs second to her sister's, it's okay provided that this response is Molly's preference because she enjoys spending time with her sister and helping her out. If, however, resentment is building up, it's not okay.

There are plenty of times in life when people extend or overextend themselves. That is not the central issue, however. Overextending yourself is not bad *provided* you do so with clear sight and a sense of choice. However, if you go against an overall sense of what seems right, feasible, or wise, the likely result will be resentment and anger. You will feel no choice in the matter. The emotional side effects will probably poison even your best efforts in the long run.

Once again we see the advantages of the Good-Enough Sibling role. The Supersibling role rarely works out well in practice. Being unconditionally available, ready to help, and always able to save the day simply exceeds human ability. Coping with troubled siblings— whether they are physically or mentally ill, drug or alcohol dependent, or affected by some other problem—leaves most Supersiblings exhausted. This can then be disruptive to their personal lives. Moreover, certain kinds of help aren't truly helpful. A troubled sibling must ultimately face his or her own problems rather than expect to be rescued. Despite good intentions, Supersiblings sometimes inadvertently augment their brothers' or sisters' difficulties. This holds true as well for less troubled siblings and their demands.

In short, the Supersibling role is often a problem in its own right. The problem is not whether to help or not; helping may or may not be appropriate. The kind and degree of help should be determined by other means. Rather, the problem is the *burdensome sense of obligation inherent in the Supersibling role*—an obligation that often creates tensions between the helper and the person being helped.

In response to this risky sense of obligation, the Good-Enough Sibling relinquishes unrealistic expectations of saving brothers and sisters. The Good-Enough Sibling strives instead to be helpful in proportion to his or her abilities and in keeping with the troubled brother's or sister's situation.

The Good-Enough Sibling is not just an abstract concept to which you can aspire; it's also a concrete set of behaviors to learn, practice, and develop. In particular, I recommend a five-step process for coming to terms with the Supersibling role and for becoming a Good-Enough Sibling—that is, moving away from a sense of burdensome, role-determined responsibility and toward a more fully conscious way of caring. Taking these steps will create changes not only for your sibling but also for you. You may, in fact, end up changing even more than your sister or brother does.

At the same time, certain forces may work against your capacity and willingness to change. One such force is denial, a defense mechanism by which your mind protects itself from unpleasant realities. If your sister is a drug abuser, for instance, the situation is hard to confront. If your brother has a psychiatric problem, it's similarly threatening. Denial puts blinders on you, thus easing the anxiety you may feel when facing challenges to your sense of the status quo. Denial is like living in a glass house: you're walled in, but you can't see the walls. The very nature of denial—and its most problematic aspect— is precisely that you don't see the problem.

But coming to terms with the situation is not made easier by denying reality. The problem is not just your troubled sibling's denial. To get beyond disappointment and pain, you must deal with your own denial as well. What everyone had always hoped would be a family member's happy, successful life turns out to be less than that—perhaps far less. In addition, you often end up having to face ingratitude, annoyance, even rage and frustration from precisely the person you're trying to help.

Furthermore, you may also have to contend with your own frustration, disappointment, and anger toward family members because of their response to you. They may get upset or reprimand you for changing your role from the Supersibling to the Good-Enough Sibling and, in so doing, no longer taking care of your brother or sister as you had before. Or they might not appreciate all you have done, and they might still expect you to provide for your sister or brother. Their responses may inadvertently reinforce your troubled sibling's reluctance to change.

There are several ways to help you overcome these situations.

To begin with, accept reality. Your brother is not necessarily the person you wish he was; however, he is simply who he is. He may not want or be able to change.

Then recognize your sibling's denial. Your sister is unable to admit the nature and extent of her problems. In fact, she doesn't even know that the problems *are* problems. Your ability to recognize that she can't see her problems is a major step.

Acknowledge the limits of your power. You cannot live your brother's life. You cannot take responsibility for choices that are his alone. Don't give unsolicited advice. Doing so may make you feel helpful, but it becomes controlling and parental. Give advice *only* when asked for it.

Finally, take charge of *your* life. All you can responsibly do is live your own life. This may well include helping your sister, but the help is most likely to be effective if it is consciously chosen and realistically matched to the circumstances.

In short, your task isn't changing your sibling but changing yourself; redefining your sibling role; ceasing to be a Supersibling and choosing to become a Good-Enough Sibling instead.

That being said, here are the five steps:

Step 1 is acknowledging that you are trying to take care of your sibling, not merely to care for him or her. You are a caretaker. You have assumed a role that is not just brotherly/sisterly but fatherly/motherly as well. Acknowledging this state of affairs is necessary before you can start to look at why you have taken on this responsibility and what it means for you.

Step 2 is finding your blind spots—looking at all the situations before you that suggest the nature of your sibling's problem and assembling them into a coherent picture. Your sister lost her job. She's in conflict with her husband. She's borrowing money. She's telling wild stories. Her appearance seems increasingly disheveled. What do these separate matters add up to? Look beyond the immediate situation. This is critical: *don't take it one situation at a time.* Cluster all the incidents that have made you say, "What's going on here?" Add them up to see the larger picture of what your sibling is doing.

Step 3 is naming your sibling's problem. Naming the problem makes it real. Without a name, the problem seems vague, all-pervasive, more threatening than it is. This is the time to call a spade a spade. "My sister is an alcoholic." "My brother is doing drugs." "She's chronically unemployed." "He's schizophrenic." "She's manic-depressive." "He's physically disabled." "She's a gambler." "He's asthmatic." "She's got an eating disorder." What I'm talking about is labeling the problem in black and white. This is applicable even if you're dealing with a sibling with ordinary problems. "He thinks he's God's gift to the world." "She thinks only her life is important." "He wants all my time and attention." Being able to name the problem you're having with your sister or brother will make it easier for you to deal with the situation.

Step 4 is becoming informed. Applicable especially to people with more severely troubled siblings, this step means gathering the facts, the data, the information—any and all available material pertaining to your brother's or sister's problem. If the problem is drugs, for instance, find books on the subject, investigate self-help groups for drug users' relatives, and learn about the illness. Do whatever is necessary to let you know what you're dealing with.

Step 5 is setting limits. This can mean a hundred and one different things. (Setting limits is discussed at length in Chapter 6.) Setting limits can mean saying yes to yourself and no to your sibling. Setting limits can mean asking "In whose best interests?" when you receive a request or demand that seems questionable or manipulative. In setting limits, you have to deal with the fear of your sibling rejecting you, getting angry because he or she resents the limits you set, or retaliating against you. However, although you take some risks when you set limits, you stand to gain as well: the benefits include emotional well-being, freedom from negative thoughts and feelings, and more energy to devote to your own activities and other relationships. What's more, by setting limits you will also be giving your sibling a chance to live his or her own life without using you as a crutch.

Here's how Dustin used the five-step process to move out of his Supersibling role and toward becoming a Good-Enough Sibling. First, Dustin realized that he was trying to take care of Kira as if he were her father rather than her brother. Second, he began to see his blind spots, which enabled him to put together previously separate incidents (Kira's work and money crises) in order to see that they were all part of a larger problem. Third, Dustin connected his sister's continual drinking with all the difficulties she had experienced, and he realized that she was an alcoholic. Fourth, he became informed about alcoholism: He attended Al-Anon meetings, read books about alcoholism, and consulted with a psychotherapist. Fifth, he then set limits on his sister's behavior.

As is typical for people trying to shed the Supersibling role, it took Dustin time to accomplish these tasks. He didn't move flawlessly from one to the next; on the contrary, it was strenuous work, and his efforts took place over the course of several crises. Dustin used these episodes to learn, to become informed about the overall situation, and to contemplate what would be most helpful.

This five-step process serves two main functions: first, it provides a means for disengaging from your siblings' unrealistic, dependent, and manipulative behavior. Second, it provides a means for devising a more conscious, perceptive form of love for your siblings.

Being a Good-Enough Sibling rather than a Supersibling does *not* mean that you cease to love your brother or sister. Quite the contrary: it means that your love can now be truly helpful. You can now devise a message of caring that encompasses realistic abilities and goals. The key factor is changing only the way you are involved in your sibling's life—*not* changing your sibling's life.

6
Setting Limits

Kalie got a frantic phone call from her sister, Allissa, when Allissa split up with her husband. Allissa had packed up and left, taking her two young sons with her. But she had no place to go.

"Can't I stay with you for a while?" Allissa pleaded.

Kalie replied, "Of course you can. Bring the kids and come right over."

Allissa soon showed up at Kalie's house with the children.

Kalie was happy to help, but the situation was difficult from the outset. Allissa doesn't drive; she had no money; she tends to be dependent anyway. "So I gave her money," Kalie explained to me in therapy. "I taught her how to drive my car so she could get around. I've put her up for weeks now, and Allissa has never even offered to help out around the house. In fact, she started complaining about my cooking. That's when I started to get angry.

"But that was only the start," Kalie went on. "Later I got a call from someone at work. They wanted me to cover the phones for half a shift—seventy-five dollars for four hours' work. I couldn't do it because I have this other job. But I wanted to help out the people who called, and I thought Allissa could use the money, so I offered her the assignment. You know what she said? 'No—tell them I'm busy.' Busy! At that point I called her a crazy fool." The two sisters ended up having a terrible argument, which concluded with Allissa packing up in tears and leaving the house.

Kalie is wrestling with a long-term sibling conflict, to be sure; but she's also wrestling with the specific issue of *limits*. "This is my sister," she told me, feeling upset. "I want to help her. I feel bad about what she's going through, and I'm trying to be good to her." Kalie feels simultaneously compassionate toward Allissa and exasperated with her. Kalie feels angry at Allissa's obstinacy and manipulative behavior, but she finds it difficult to express her anger without feeling heartless. She wants to do "enough" and be a Good-Enough Sibling but she isn't sure what that is. The uncertainty causes her great worry and emotional discomfort. She can't figure out how to make herself available without wrenching her own life apart. She doesn't know how to help Allissa when Allissa won't even help herself. Kalie feels she's stuck, with no good course of action before her.

Kalie's situation with Allissa is complex and intense, but the core issues aren't at all unusual. Many people find themselves caught up in their siblings' problems and feel uncertain about how and when to try solving them. Time after time I hear my patients express concerns like these: "I get so confused. Maybe it's me—maybe I should be more willing to give. Is it right for me to hold the line when my sister asks for more than I can give? Am I holding back too much from her? Should I resist her demands on me?" The specific circumstances take any number of shapes. Is it advisable to loan a sibling money? What sorts of other resources should one offer—a place to stay, for instance? And what about advice: is it proper to urge a brother or sister toward a certain course of action? These are the kinds of issues that crop up in the pursuit of being a Good-Enough Sibling, all of which concern the question of unconditional availability, which I discussed in Chapter 4. How much is *enough*? And what is *too* much?

How do you actualize being a Good-Enough Sibling, who is caring, responsive, and attentive to your brothers and sisters? How do you avoid the Supersibling trap of being too caring, too responsive, and too attentive? What constitutes help that truly helps your sibling instead of damages his or her self-reliance and self-esteem? What fosters mutual respect and concern rather than mutual dependency?

Setting limits is at the heart of these issues. Setting limits is a way of expressing a practical, tough-minded love for your sibling and, simultaneously, a way of charting territory as a Good-Enough Sibling. Although limits may be difficult to set, setting them in some way or other is inevitable. If your brother wants to borrow your car, for instance, you won't lend it to him forever. You'll limit the loan to some degree: an hour, a day, a week, whatever.

Setting limits therefore consists of finding the most appropriate and creative line between what you will and won't accept in your relationships. For example, Nora's sister Jillian would often call to chat about the day's events. While Nora welcomed her sister's conversation, she sometimes found the calls inconvenient and disruptive. How long could she tolerate these constant interruptions? She soon found it unacceptable to have Jillian take up one or two hours of her evening. Jillian called one night when Nora had already made plans. "I'd love to talk, but I can't right now," Nora said. "Let me call you back in a couple of hours." Jillian was furious—so offended that she wouldn't talk to Nora for almost two weeks. For Nora, the challenge was determining what felt tolerable and what felt intolerable, then coming up with an alternate plan that took her feelings as well as Jillian into account.

Remember: *however long you choose to tolerate a difficult sibling situation without setting limits, that is how long you* will *tolerate it.* Ultimately the choice is yours.

Setting limits is a technique you can employ for both major and minor problems. It involves putting boundaries in place—boundaries that protect both you and your sibling. These boundaries are effective in all kinds of situations. Whether you have a deeply troubled sibling or merely a sibling with troubles, setting limits will serve you well in reshaping your relationship. This process in turn will help you reshape your concept of yourself as a Good-Enough Sibling.

Limit setting is difficult because most people mistake it for rejection. This is true both for you as the setter of limits and for your sibling as the person whose behavior ends up limited. "But I thought you cared!" your sister shouts. "I didn't think you'd be so selfish!" your brother snaps. It's not at all uncommon for troubled siblings to see your limits as signs that you've ceased to love them and help them with their troubles.

In fact, nothing could be further from the truth. Setting limits is not the end of *caring for* your sibling; rather, setting limits is the end of *taking care of* your sibling. Setting limits is the process of finding and expressing a new way of caring—a way that supports and encourages your sibling's efforts to take care of himself or herself. Limits do not prevent you from caring; what they prevent is your getting entangled in your sibling's troubles. In fact, setting limits enables you to provide support and encouragement in a far more caring way than you might without the limits in place.

The reasons aren't hard to detect. When you take care of people— when you intercede for them in ways that substitute your insights, decisions, and actions for their own—you may end up feeling angry and resentful over the efforts you must exert on their behalf because you feel manipulated, taken advantage of, coerced, or even forced into these actions. As a result, the actions you take in these situations often end up intermingled with your anger and resentment. By contrast, when you care for someone, you're freer to express a kind of love untainted by these hostile emotions.

Ironically, limits often increase rather than decrease a sense of freedom—your freedom to live your own life, certainly, but also your freedom to offer genuine assistance to your sister or brother without aiding and abetting her or his self-defeating behaviors.

This is not to say, however, that setting limits is easy or pleasant. Both you and your sister or brother will probably find the process difficult and stressful, perhaps even painful. When you set limits for your siblings, you may feel as if you're pushing them into a lake; on the contrary, what you're doing is giving them the opportunity to swim by themselves. If you continue to drag them along emotionally and financially, they'll remain unable to survive on their own. In effect, *not* setting limits helps them live a life of dependency and low self-esteem. And it is precisely this belief that you must relinquish: that you are indispensable. Unbeknownst to you, feeling so needed and depended upon may be the glue that keeps you so involved. You have to be prepared to find another way of feeling needed and important, so that you can let your brother or sister survive without you.

Essentially I'm saying that when you set limits you give your siblings an important element of freedom. Of course, the complicating factor is that they don't *want* the freedom. And there's a good chance that when you set the limits, they'll attack you for your audacity in thrusting freedom on them. To them, your efforts feel like rejection; their sensation is not of swimming but of drowning.

So what makes all this bearable? What makes it feasible? One of my patients, Lisa, posed the quandary she faces with her sister: "How much do I give? I either give too much or not at all. How do I find the happy medium?"

How to Set Limits

There are essentially three steps to setting limits on your sibling's unreasonable expectations or behavior.

Step 1 is taking a pulse on how you're feeling. The most common indicators that you have insufficient limits in place are feelings of anger or resentment, of being taken advantage of, disregarded, unappreciated, manipulated, controlled, or treated as unimportant. Any one of these feelings *in excess* suggests that your efforts may be out of proportion to your sibling's situation. The presence of two or more is all the more significant. Minor flare-ups aren't necessarily a problem—we all have moments of exasperation toward siblings. But long-term, intense emotions of this sort are another matter.

Take your frustrations seriously. They are a sign that you probably need to set some limits. Note, too, that the emotions themselves are not the problem; they are a symptom of something beneath the surface. Anger and resentment are, in fact, protentially creative feelings. They are catalysts for change. They are indications that your sibling relationship needs transformation or, at the very least, some serious tinkering.

In the story that opened this chapter, for example, Kalie felt nearly all the emotions mentioned here: angry, resentful, taken advantage of, treated as unappreciated and unimportant. She was seething with exasperation over her conflict with Allissa. Why? Because Kalie was trying to do too much for her sister.

Once you know how you're feeling, *Step 2 is identifying the source of these feelings*. Let's go back to Kalie. What angered her was that she was going to bat for her sister without her sister making the slightest effort on her own behalf. Not only had Allissa failed to appreciate Kalie's efforts to find her some work but she had also failed to take any initiative to help herself. Kalie felt that she was giving or doing everything she could, yet Allissa wasn't doing anything for herself and was unappreciative of what she was getting. This situation alerted Kalie to the fact that she was carrying too much responsibility for Allissa. "If Allissa won't carry her own weight," Kalie soon asked herself, "why should I?"

Now comes *Step 3: figuring out where you want to set the limit, then setting it*. Taking this step means asking yourself, "How much do I want to give, and how much feels burdensome or excessive?" Kalie, for example, felt that her sister was having a problem and that she wanted to help. Fine. But if Allissa was in a fix, did Kalie have to do *everything* in her power to help? Was Kalie obligated to solve *all* Allissa's problems? And did she have to solve them even if Allissa herself seemed unable or unwilling to take action? Kalie overextended herself, got angry, and wound up throwing Allissa out of the house. Her best intentions went awry. If she'd been able to set limits on her availability from the start (such as saying, "You can stay here two weeks; then you have to move"), her efforts to be helpful could have been realized. Kalie made many resources—money, work, lodging— available, yet her sister not only wasn't taking advantage of them but wasn't doing anything to develop her own resources.

The key to limit setting is accepting a manageable slice of the situation you face rather than the whole pie. This is true in dealing with a barrage of demands from your sister or brother but even more true when dealing with a Supersibling situation. If you are a Supersibling, part of your task is realizing that what you do may be helpful but not necessarily curative. That is, your help may make a contribution to your sibling's well-being but not settle all his or her problems once and for all. Consider the possibility of doing *something* rather than *everything*. You needn't throw yourself completely into the situation.

First of all, you're only human. You can't really solve someone else's problems. You can provide certain kinds of assistance: advice, emotional support, financial help. Even offering everything you have—every brilliant insight, every bit of compassion, every last penny—isn't likely to solve all the difficulties your sibling may encounter. In short, your ordinary and forgiveable human limitations constrain what you can do for someone else.

Second, you can't help your sibling (or anyone else) if you make a shambles of your own life in the process. Giving time, effort, and money to the people you love is all well and good, but doing so to the degree that you damage your health, sanity, or financial stability will backfire. It will wreck your own life *and* your ability to help your sibling. In the words of an old adage, you can't save someone who's drowning if you yourself can't swim.

Third, you can't live your sibling's life. Your brother must face his own responsibilities; your sister must take hold of her own problems. By attempting to do everything to help, you may actually jeopardize your sibling's attempt to make sense of life, to get a handle on issues, to solve problems. The effort to do everything for your brother or sister may ultimately damage his or her chances for personal growth.

In the situation discussed in Chapter 5, Dustin explained to his sister Kira that he was setting three limits in their relationship. She would have to move out within a month. During her remaining stay, she could not drink while in the house. And she could not depend on Dustin for transportation to her job. Kira argued against these restrictions but ended up complying with them. She didn't drink at Dustin's place; she found someone to drive her to work; and she moved out three weeks later. Having set these limits, Dustin felt an enormous sense of relief. Setting limits not only preserved his relationship with Kira but also prevented what was becoming a major marital conflict. As Dustin's wife, Eve, put it: "If he hadn't put some sort of limits on Kira, the situation would have destroyed our marriage."

The upshot of all this is fairly straightforward. Depending on what emotions you feel and on what your feelings suggest as directions for change, you can take specific actions that help your sibling without depleting your own energy and patience. This process is not necessarily easy. In fact, it can be quite difficult, especially if your sister or brother is in a state of intense emotional need. But the process is easier than most of the alternatives, including that of taking excessive, unrealistic actions that can complicate your sibling's life as well as your own.

On some level, setting limits always means saying no. No to repeated requests for money. No to unreasonable expectations of time and attention. No to demands for unending emotional support. This is part of what makes setting limits difficult: we all find it hard to say no. Yet the willingness to say no is at the heart of this task. This doesn't necessarily mean a categorical, across-the-board *no*. It's often a qualified no. It's a no that limits what you'll give your sibling, when, how, and under what circumstances. What is realistic for you to do? What is feasible for you? This is the starting point.

To say no to others, you have to know yourself. That's really the core of being able to set a limit. You have to know what is upsetting you, what is taxing you, what is antagonistic to you. Then, instead of taking responsibility for your sibling, you have to take responsibility for how *you* feel.

Here's another example. One of my patients, Marcy, was planning a big holiday dinner for friends. She called Nadia, her sister, to invite her and her husband. Marcy had felt frustrated with Nadia and her husband, Adrian, for a long time, because they never reciprocated her invitations. Even so, she wanted them present if they chose to come. Marcy set the time and made the dinner.

Several days in advance, Nadia called Marcy and said, "Can't you make it some night other than Friday? Adrian wants to work late that evening, so it's not a good time for him." Marcy was furious. Not only had she extended herself to make the dinner, now she was being hassled about the time. In the past, this sort of situation had prompted Marcy to react in one of two extreme ways. Either she rejected her sister and refused any contact with her or she responded to her demands and did everything possible to smooth over the situation.

Through therapy, however, we had worked on this issue. Marcy followed the three steps for limit setting. First, she took a pulse on how she felt and realized that she felt angry, taken advantage of, resentful, and unappreciated. Second, she identified the source of her feelings: her sister's being unaware of Marcy's efforts and inconsiderate toward her needs. Third, she determined where she could set the limit—that is, what she could do without feeling pushed over the line. And she decided that she'd make dinner without juggling the schedule to suit her sister and brother-in-law.

Subsequently, she told Nadia and Adrian, "This is when I'm making dinner. If you want to come, you're welcome to join us. If you can't come, then perhaps we'll see you next time." Marcy succeeded in finding a middle course. She said no but also yes. She extended her hospitality without acting like a doormat. She was firm in not complying with last-minute rearrangements. Having invited many other guests, Marcy wasn't going to change the night just to accommodate her sister and her husband.

When Nadia called back, she apologized, saying, "Sorry for the inconvenience. We'd like to come, so we'll be there." Nadia had seen the limit and responded to it.

Marcy's decision and subsequent actions illustrate the importance and usefulness of a clearly set limit. Unless you are specific about how far you'll let people push you, they'll push you as far as they can. However, when you are able to put up a specific stop sign—as Marcy did—many people will respond.

Implicit in the issue of saying no is clear communication. When you draw the line, make sure you do so clearly. Vague or poorly expressed limits are almost as bad as none at all, since your sibling won't know where the limits are. The risk of vague messages is that your sister or brother will misunderstand what you've said, with the result of further bad feeling.

Frank, for instance, has received many requests for financial help from his brother Jed. Many years ago Frank loaned Jed large sums of cash. Jed paid the money back but took his time, with hard feelings almost always flaring up between the brothers. Frank considered the possibility of not loaning Jed any money, but he rejected that idea because Jed lived a precarious life; these periodic infusions of cash had prevented disaster more than once. Yet Frank also resented Jed's reliance on him as a one-man loan department. Why couldn't Jed pull himself together enough to handle his finances better?

At some point, Frank stumbled into a solution. He'd loan Jed money, but only in small quantities, and only as a last resort. Frank told his brother that he'd lend him cash in a real jam—but only a hundred dollars. That seemed enough to get Jed through any given emergency, but it wasn't so much that Jed could rely on Frank to solve his problems. The loans were a crisis fund but nothing more.

Frank had followed the three steps described earlier. He sized up his own frustration (anger at Jed), identified its source (repeated requests for money), and set a limit (loans of only a hundred dollars, and only as a last resort).

Frank's course of action seemed to help both Jed and Frank himself. But it worked in part because the limit Frank set was clear. He didn't refuse outright to loan Jed any money. Jed might have taken that as a total rejection, which wasn't what Frank intended or what Jed could have handled. Neither did Frank simply say, "Well, I'll lend you some money, but not very much." Jed could have interpreted that offer through the distorted lens of his financial need. "Not very much" might have meant a thousand dollars to Jed, even ten thousand. Instead, Frank put his offer in specific terms. One hundred dollars— period. The only way Frank could have been more precise (and perhaps helpfully so) would have been to clarify the timing of his offers. "I'll lend you money, but only a hundred dollars, no more than twice a year, and you'll repay each loan within six months." Still, the limits Frank set seem to work. Jed takes him up on his offer now and then, but otherwise seems to have pulled himself together financially. The brothers remain close; a major irritant between them is now absent.

The most significant reason for setting limits is that when you put a "brake" on how much you make yourself available, you won't have to "break" the relationship. What you may not realize is that in setting a limit you're protecting your sister or brother from your own anger, which might ultimately damage the relationship. You're taking care of yourself, but you're also caring for your sibling *in the long run*. By refusing to indulge your brother's or sister's short-term whims (for money, attention, help, and so on), you're also taking care of the relationship. In a sense you're offering more of yourself in the long run by rationing yourself in the short run. You're doing what you can to pace yourself, thus avoiding a big explosion of the sort that often occurs when one sibling demands too much of another. You're trying to guarantee your sister or brother that you'll stay involved without reaching a point where the relationship becomes oppressive.

People get thrown off balance in setting limits by taking on not only their half of the bargain but their siblings' as well. "How am I going to get him to follow the limits?" they ask. "I made myself clear, but my brother still doesn't see the point." What if Katie had explained that she'd put her sister, Allissa, up for a week, but not indefinitely, and Allissa had still demanded a long-term stay?

One of the most important things to realize is that you are not responsible for getting your sibling to follow the limit. You *are* responsible for following it yourself, and for reinforcing it. That is, to set a limit effectively you have to be ready to change your own behavior, not your sibling's. This is the focal point of setting limits—and without question the hardest part.

When you set a limit and stop taking care of your siblings, there may be an interim during which they plummet before pulling themselves together and beginning to assume their own responsibilities. Depending on the severity of the problems involved, you must be prepared for your siblings to hit bottom. They may lose their jobs, end up broke, or have nowhere to live. Yet this situation, however hard to watch, may be what they need to decide at last to change without expecting someone else to do it for them. Even if they don't pick up their responsibilities right away, even if they end up floundering for a while, this is where you need to hold the line. No matter how hard to watch, their situation may be the catalyst for change that they've needed.

When Allissa asked Kalie to put her up indefinitely, the request frustrated and annoyed Kalie. If Kalie had refused her sister eternal room and board, Allissa would probably have gotten angry at her. But her anger would not have obligated Kalie to violate the limit she'd set. She had set it; now she should keep it. If you have a comparable situation, you should keep your share of any bargain even if your sibling doesn't keep his or hers.

The essence of this situation is that when you're dealing with siblings in need, they know only their needs—and often only their needs at that moment. In many instances, they're not going to remember what you discussed. No matter how much you anticipate their responses, no matter how clearly you set the limit, they may come back later as if for the first time: "But why can't you put me up for the next couple of months?" In short, your task is setting the limit and keeping to your half of the bargain. You can't *make* your siblings understand. Your responsibility is not to force their perception of reality (which in fact they may not see at all) but to hold on to reality yourself.

Kinds of Limits

Setting limits doesn't necessarily mean that you refuse to do something. It may mean that you do something in a new or different way, or to a different degree. The previous examples are useful but almost too tidy, since money and even housing are much easier to quantify than other "goods" you may choose to share with your siblings. Here are some other—and often more intangible—examples.

You can set limits by changing your availability. If your sibling needs

94

your advice or emotional support, for instance, you can limit the times (or the length of time) you're available. You might end up telling your brother, "I'll talk with you about your problems at work, but we have to limit our conversations to an hour each week." Or you may end up specifying *when* you are available: "I can't talk with you when you call right at dinnertime, but Sunday evenings should work out all right."

You can set limits by *suggesting alternatives instead of giving more direct assistance.* If you're not in a position to help your sister with loans or advice, you may be at least as helpful—perhaps even more so—by suggesting ways she can help herself or find help elsewhere. If she's plagued by money problems, for example, you might say, "Why don't you talk with those financial counseling centers the city has set up?" If she has an alcohol problem, you might ask, "Have you considered going to Alcoholics Anonymous?" You can offer suggestions without trying to be your sibling's rescuer. Don't get in over your head. Just as you wouldn't operate on your brother even if you were a trained surgeon, you shouldn't take on the roles of financial adviser, lawyer, or psychotherapist without sufficient knowledge. Offer possibilities, not panaceas.

You can set limits by *disengaging from your sibling's dependence.* Your sister's reliance on you does not obligate you to solve her problems. On the contrary, her reliance may be the problem itself. One of the most important limits you can set is your disengagement from excessive dependence. As you offer alternatives of the sorts suggested in the previous paragraph, emphasize that choosing among them is your sibling's responsibility. "Here are some different things you can do—but the choice of which to do is *yours.*" Draw the line in terms of how much you are responsible.

Finally, you can set limits by *declining to rescue your sibling.* This is one of the hardest tasks before you: knowing when your "help" may do more damage than good. If your brother wants money for drugs or liquor, granting his request does him no favor at all. If your sister wants you to support her, the free ride may be just the opposite of what she needs. Sometimes your outright refusal to cooperate is ultimately the kindest act—though your sibling will think otherwise, and will probably tell you so.

What sorts of situations are typically fair game for applying these guidelines? Of course, any number of issues crop up, and they vary from family to family. But the most common are those that depend on availability of time and money.

Perhaps you feel that your sibling wants too much of your time to hash over personal problems. Even if you genuinely want to help, you may feel exhausted by the demands on you as a sounding board, counselor, or adviser. The problem is twofold: the quantity of time spent in conversation and the content of the dialogue.

The issue of time is frustrating but relatively easy to address. You can contain demands on your time much as you can contain demands on your money.

First, decide how much you have to spare.

Second, express the limits that you're setting in clear terms.

Third, keep to the limits.

You might, for example, decide that you'll talk with your sibling half an hour every other day (or one hour a week, or one hour a month—whatever you choose). State the limit firmly but gently: "I'll be happy to talk with you, but you know how hectic it is around here, so we'll have to keep it down to forty minutes, okay?" Then stick to your guns.

A variation on this theme is dealing with phone calls. If your sister or brother is needing a lot of your attention, the phone can become an instrument of torture. For this reason, you shouldn't hesitate to structure phone calls. Indicate in advance that you have only a limited time to talk, If your sibling's call has come at an inconvenient moment, say so. If you agree to talk but the conversation goes on too long, indicate that time is up. Say, "I have to go in five minutes." If your sibling pleads, "But I'm not done yet!" then explain, "I know we're in the middle of something, but we're really going to have to pick up on this tomorrow. I'll call you back." Be firm and consistent.

The issue of content is more complex. Are you feeling that your sibling is putting you on the spot by inappropriate requests for advice or help? Is he or she using you as a scapegoat or go-between? Here again you have to size up what you have to offer, decide on a limit, express it, and enforce it. You can give a very clear message about what you will and will not listen to. For example, if two of your sisters are angry at one another and you feel drawn into the conflict when one of them calls you, you can respond like this: "Look, I care about you, but it's too hurtful to me to hear you go on about each other. This is *your* argument. I don't want to get caught in the cross fire; I'm close to both of you. *You* solve the problem." Don't let yourself be put in untenable positions.

Perhaps the biggest single sore spot is (predictably) money. If your sibling is in a financial fix, you're probably one of the first persons he or she is likely to ask for help.

Should you help? That's your decision. Certainly there are times when financial assistance is appropriate. But think through the following questions before you help.

First, how much financial responsibility are you prepared to take for our brother's or sister's life? Some people are quite happy to help out generously. If you are—and if your resources permit—your generosity may be appropriate. However, a big loan or gift may not be what your sibling needs. Will the money pull your brother out of his problem—or simply allow him to postpone a real solution? Will a loan help your sister get her life organized—or fragment it further? Will a gift boost your brother's sagging morale—or demoralize him further? Will money help your sister be less dependent—or make her all the more so?

Second, there's a consideration closer to home. What will your financial assistance do to you? One of my patients, for instance, was prepared to take all her money out of the bank and give it to her sister. This savings was to have been her tuition for graduate school. Would undercutting her own education have served her well in the long run? If giving to your sister or brother jeopardizes your own health or well-being, there's a problem.

The core issue is this: will your financial assistance truly help? Or will it only make it easy for your sibling to postpone dealing with his or her real problems? Loans and gifts that reinforce a troubled sibling's self-delusion—whether the problem is alcoholism, drug abuse, compulsive gambling, chronic unemployment, or some other serious personal difficulty—ultimately do your sibling a grave disservice.

As the intricacy of this discussion suggests, setting limits is a complex and emotionally sensitive issue. It's not easy to do; it's not fun; it takes a clear sense of purpose and resolution. Still, it's a critical step to take when your siblings are troubled and your relationships with them are, too.

Your sibling in need may pressure you in ways that intensify your sense of guilt and anguish over his or her personal troubles. He or she may yell at you, get angry, and blame you when you set your limit. How, then, do you handle this barrage so that you don't get derailed from setting your limit? The key is to *respond* to what your sibling is saying to you rather than *react* to the content of what he or she is saying.

If you can avoid reacting to your sibling's attacks, demands, criticisms, accusations, or emotional outbursts with counterattacks, counterdemands, countercriticisms, and so forth, you will be able to stay focused on your objectives and follow through on setting limits. The hardest task you must accomplish is to avoid getting dragged into the upheaval of your own anger or your sibling's. Don't get caught up in the particulars of why he feels angry at you. Remember that setting a limit is a way to protect yourself better. You're beginning to fend for yourself so that you don't constantly have to defend yourself or explain your behavior. Stay focused on the limits you have decided to set; relate to your sibling simply by acknowledging his distress with you. This will enable you to respond calmly rather than react angrily or defensively to what he's saying.

Here's a sequence of steps to take so you can respond calmly rather than react heatedly to your sibling: first, observe your sibling's reaction to what you've said; second, reflect it back in a caring, empathic way; third, carry on with your message without getting caught up in your sibling's attack on you or defending yourself against the accusations.

Here's an example. Kelly's sister, Melanie, often stopped by in the afternoon, stayed for dinner, then lingered as long as she wished. Kelly found that these visits interfered with her evening routines. For this reason, Kelly set a limit: Melanie could come, but she had to leave by 9:00 P.M. Melanie resented this constraint and attacked Kelly, dragging up all sorts of issues from the sisters' past, including "You always had an easier time with Mom than I did." Although taken aback by these accusations, Kelly didn't react; instead, she observed that Melanie was upset, and she said, "I understand that you're really angry with me. But despite what you're saying, I'm not doing this because I don't care for you. I really *do* care." After reassuring her sister, Kelly followed through in setting her limit: "You're welcome here, but from now on you'll have to leave by nine."

If you attempt to answer every point a troubled sibling raises, you'll inevitably end up lost. Every point that troubled siblings make is an extension of how they feel. They feel cheated and deprived. They feel needy. No matter how hard you try, *you'll never succeed in reasoning away their needs or their feelings*. It simply can't be done. You'll come away not only frustrated but guilty. How can you say no when they're so needy!

Another pitfall in setting limits is getting caught up in the past. When sorting out these issues of availability and responsibility, many of us fall back into childhood sibling roles. We get stuck in our old "seats" and can't get out. For instance, Gordon finds himself in a recurrent drama with his brother Russ:

"When I go around and around with my brother, we sometimes fall into our old pattern—the dependent little brother wanting the more competent older brother to help him out. It's hard not to. There's a gravitational pull that's always tugging at us." However, as Gordon has learned to set limits with Russ, he's grasped the obvious: They are no longer little boys stuck in unchangeable patterns of behavior. "Whatever the past was, things are different now. We're adults, and I need to constrain him partly for my own sanity and partly for his own well-being. Part of what I do is to pull myself back from falling into the same old traps. There's still the temptation, but far less than before. We don't have to play that game anymore. And if Russ wants to, *I* still don't have to."

Finally, there's the issue of exhaustion. Plenty of competent women and men simply reach a point of having no more energy left to expend on their siblings' problems. They don't necessarily feel angry, resentful, or hostile; they've simply run out of steam. Emotional depletion of this sort is a problem but can also be a potential turning point. What happens when your sister or brother has worn you out? Perhaps that's the final writing on the wall. You've done everything you can, and maybe more than you should have. *Now* what? Well, maybe nothing. Maybe it's not even possible to do something more. You can't help it if you're completely depleted. What I mean to suggest is that part of setting limits is finding your own depletion level. Just as anger can indicate a problem you're attempting to ignore, so can exhaustion.

What's happening when you feel that your brother's or sister's problems have left you dead on your feet?

You're really hearing two messages. One is that you've probably done too much. You're overextended. Rather than a Good-Enough Sibling, you've been a Supersibling. For your own sanity and health (not to mention those of your spouse, children, and friends), you should cut back in some way. You have to set more limits.

The second message is that you have to take the long view. This ties in with what I said earlier about putting on the brakes to avoid a break. Your sibling relationships may last for the rest of your life. If you pace yourself, you're actually more likely to be helpful than if you burn out and either can't deal with the situation any longer or just run out of energy or the desire to help.

Many of my patients are working hard to come to terms with sibling conflicts. Some of them have deeply troubled brothers or sisters; others have brothers or sisters who aren't especially troubled but whose relationships present problems. Either way, my patients often find themselves struggling with the task of setting limits. In doing so, a lot of them gradually develop a stronger sense of themselves and of what it means to be a Good-Enough Sibling. My patients and their siblings ultimately benefit from this process. As I've stressed, it's difficult getting there, but the difficulty doesn't mean that the task shouldn't be undertaken.

In setting limits with siblings, many people feel an alarming sense of aloneness. This isn't surprising. In a very real sense they are separating from previous sorts of involvement with family members; they experience a real loss as they relinquish old familiar assumptions, roles, and patterns of behavior. Along with this relinquishment come the feelings that accompany any loss: emptiness, anxiety, and fear.

Do these feelings mean that setting limits is too difficult? Do they mean that being a Good-Enough Sibling is too dangerous?

Not at all. On the contrary, the emptiness, anxiety, and fear my patients describe are normal growing pains. You are changing, developing, and moving beyond old habits and expectations. These transitions are not easy.

So what's the surprise that the changes you experience as a certified, card-carrying adult should knock you around a bit? These growing pains, like those at other stages of life, are a good sign. In fact, the discomfort you feel in growing into a more clear-sighted, autonomous person means you're taking steps forward. You shouldn't let these pains alarm you. Tolerate them; they will pass.

One last aspect of this situation needs to be mentioned. What about the guilt that setting limits may prompt you to feel? What does this say about what you've done to your siblings?

Here again I'd like to underscore something mentioned earlier simply because it's so important. Setting limits doesn't mean you stop loving your siblings; it only means you're expressing love in a different way. The limits themselves are an expression of your love. Look at it as the difference between conditional and unconditional availability. Up till now, your sisters or brothers have demanded that you be unconditionally available: ready at any time to meet their needs for support and help. What you need to establish is conditional availability: you will be ready to help when the help is appropriate and constructive. Is this a diminishment of love? Not at all. The love you feel can be the same, or even more intense; you're just expressing it in a more specific, well-considered way.

Keep these points in mind as you set the limits for your sibling:

Setting limits takes practice. Often you can set limits only with repeated efforts; like other aspects of dealing with people, setting limits is a skill you have to learn. The only way to determine where to set a limit may be to go through the process of setting it a few times. This actually helps you clarify your objective and modify your limits till you find your comfort zone.

Deciding to set limits and beginning to do so are a major accomplishment. Although setting limits is a challenging task, you have already fought half the battle simply by recognizing its necessity and beginning the process.

You have to persist in your efforts to set limits once you've begun. Don't get frustrated, angry with yourself, or disheartened simply because you don't succeed right off or after several tries. The fact that you have begun to set limits speaks well for your chances for eventual success. You may not have the emotional follow-through at the outset to reach the goal you seek; however, this energy will come in the long run. You will ultimately actualize your limit. Don't worry about consistency; this will follow in time. Just work on clarifying your limits and starting the limit setting itself.

The Care Package

Dorothy had always been dependent on her older sister, Margaret. During adulthood, this dependence included Dorothy's expectations that Margaret would rescue her during any of Dorothy's chronic financial problems. Margaret gradually grew angry and resentful about always having to be there for her sister's crises—to listen to her, to give her advice, and especially to send her money.

In reaching her own explosion point, Margaret realized that she had to set some limits on her sister's demands. The task wasn't easy. Margaret had a rough time deciding what to do. She ultimately decided to limit the times her sister could call her so that she wouldn't continue to be wakened in the middle of the night. She also decided that she would no longer send her sister money. Margaret told Dorothy of these limits, but her sister didn't believe her. Dorothy accused Margaret of being indifferent—even of wanting her to suffer. Shaken by these accusations, Margaret faltered; she stated her intentions but didn't always follow through; she adjusted the terms of the limits several times. Yet Margaret continued to feel that setting limits made sense and that she could succeed in doing so. She wanted to be supportive of Dorothy but knew she couldn't be there for her all the time in all ways. Setting limits provided her with an alternative way of giving: something rather than everything or nothing.

Over the months, the situation improved. Dorothy stablized her life and balanced her budget; she even accepted Margaret's limits on when she could call. In fact, since Margaret set the limits, her sister's problems have subsided. Dorothy has begun to face her own situation more squarely. And the sisters are getting along better than before.

"In the past, when my sister was always in a fix and running out of money," Margaret explains, "I'd immediately offer her a loan. At some point I realized that in our family the only way we ever showed support was to give money. It wasn't what we necessarily wanted or needed; that's just what we did. And money wasn't helping Dorothy face her problems. So at some point I told her I couldn't give her any more money, but I'd listen to her and be supportive of her. She wasn't thrilled, but she accepted the limits I'd set."

Something else worked out too. "A few months later, I decided to send her a 'care package.' I got this box and put in some of the things that my sister really loves. I put in a book she likes, a special kind of candy, and some other things. And for the first time, I felt that without sending money I was able to let her know I loved her."

7

Sibling "Cold Wars"

What awful grievance must occur to prompt a brother to disown his brother? What event would compel a sister to stop talking to her sister for months, even years? Why do siblings reach such drastic misunderstandings that they see no alternative but to sever all communication and declare a kind of sibling "cold war"? How do these cold wars occur? And why do they often last so long?

This phenomenon isn't at all unusual; on the contrary, it's distressingly common. Many sisters and brothers experience conflicts so severe that they cut off contact or wall each other out. The ensuing silence isn't necessarily permanent—it may last a few days, a week or two, or several months—but it's hurtful and confusing all the same; and in some instances the hostilities can last for years, for decades, even for a lifetime.

These cold wars are one of the most extreme expressions of sibling rivalry. Precisely because of their severity and relative frequency, however, they deserve special attention.

What Are Sibling Cold Wars?

Sibling cold wars are serious ruptures in a relationship in which one sibling grows angry with another and can't discuss either the anger or its sources. Not only are the siblings unable to talk—they don't know how to talk and refuse to talk. The anger and its expression are central to their state of mind. The anger is their most compelling need—more important than its causes or any possible solutions. Anger of this sort is often self-perpetuating.

Sibling cold wars aren't simply a matter of brothers and sisters growing apart. Many sisters and brothers grow apart in a peaceful, mutually agreed-upon way. They may or may not feel regret or sadness that they're not closer, but they hold little or no animosity toward one another. There's simply a lack of common ground or a relatively weak bond between them. By contrast, the sibling cold war is an active, angry rejection of one sibling by another. So there's a crucial distinction between siblings who drift apart and siblings who force each other away deliberately. The essence of the sibling cold war isn't indifference but *anger*. One sibling takes offense at something and rejects the other. The second sibling retaliates or at least gets pulled into this standoff. Either they react with mutual anger and won't communicate or one sibling retreats for self-protection until an overture to restore some measure of harmony is made.

Sheila and Eileen are close in some ways, but they have a tempestuous and increasingly brittle relationship. Whenever Sheila expresses any anger toward her sister, Eileen ices her out. Eileen refuses to have anything to do with Sheila; she rebuffs all efforts at communication; she acts almost as if Sheila is dead, buried, and forgotten. Sitting down and talking with Sheila about their troubles is an alien concept to Eileen. She can't imagine even wanting to do it. The sisters' anger is the cause of war; once started, the war rages till it simply burns itself out.

These sisters' cold wars last for months or years at a time, ending only when Sheila makes some sort of overture to Eileen. At such points, the women bridge the gap without discussion of what had happened; they proceed as if nothing at all took place; and they resume having good times together. But their relationship is a time bomb that will go off again before long.

What triggered it this time is that Sheila made a lunch date with

Eileen, but she forgot a prior commitment and needed to reschedule. Sheila called Eileen to explain the situation. But Eileen took offense and accused her sister of not having time for her. When the discussion seemed to be going nowhere, Sheila said, "Look, I'm really tired— let's talk about this tomorrow." Eileen took further offense: "You don't even care enough to sort out the mess you've made!" she yelled, then hung up. Eileen's feelings were so badly hurt that she froze her sister out yet again; another cold war began.

As the two oldest sons in a family of six children, Tod and Wayne have both carried heavy responsibilities and gained high respect among their siblings. Both men are accomplished and strong-willed, yet their styles and goals are different: Tod is an easygoing, nurturing high-school teacher; Wayne is ambitious, even aggressive, in his pursuit of a business career.

Tod and Wayne clash frequently over politics, religion, finances, artistic values, and issues of personal life-style. But an underlying disagreement causes more problems than their outward differences of opinion. Tod sees life as a series of necessary and often congenial compromises. Wayne sees life as a series of battles over abstract principles. If the brothers differ in opinion, Wayne grows increasingly rigid; when Tod tries to ease the tensions by offering to compromise, Wayne grows even more irate. He accuses his brother of being wishy-washy as well as wrong. Soon Tod feels hemmed in—Wayne has backed him up against the wall. The brothers usually engage in a final argument before falling silent.

Weeks or months later, when one or the other grows weary of the situation or some family incident (such as their mother's chronic illness) requires their collaboration, they get in touch again. But another blowup is inevitable. Knowing that does nothing to ease the tensions between these brothers; on the contary, the sense of impending trouble leaves them both wary, weary, and irritable.

The Causes of Cold War

These stories could easily have involved a brother and a sister or some combination of several siblings of either sex. (Cold wars in which brothers and sisters take sides in alliances aren't as common as one-to-one combat, but they do occur.) What's significant about these tales could apply to most sibling cold wars. Both involve a history of sibling conflict, sibling rivalry, smoldering anger or resentment, and poor communication.

All siblings have squabbles, of course, most conspicuously while growing up. Many of these clashes revolve around a multitude of situations that breed jealousy, competition, and resentment. Still others result from differences in each brother's or sister's Good-Enough Sibling ideal. The siblings have different expectations of proper behavior toward each other; as a result, they may feel angry or disappointed about not getting the treatment they feel they deserve. In this sense, the Good-Enough Sibling ideal—or, rather, the many variations on this ideal that individual sisters and brothers hold—lies at the heart of sibling cold wars.

In addition, however, some sisters and brothers seem especially volatile toward each other—quicker to take offense, more strident in their accusations, less patient with the ups and downs of their relationships. Is the problem that these siblings tend to fight more easily or often than others? Ironically, sisters and brothers who argue often may be *less* prone to cold wars; their ability to put problems on the table may serve as a vent to release accumulating tensions. Such siblings have differences, but they acknowledge them and work them out.

By contrast, some siblings who put a high premium on harmony at all costs, and whose history thus involves *ignoring* conflicts, may be prone to cut each other off. These siblings may find that changes in their respective roles are threatening. Therefore, the cold war can be a way of trying to thwart change, which often has potentially negative side effects. Additionally, cold wars are sometimes waged because one sibling has an extensive list of grievances that leads to ongoing strife.

The problem is that they have suppressed conflicts so often that they continue to do so by habit rather than to work toward resolving their misunderstandings.

Siblings who frequently end up in conflict may feel scant toward each other between battles: they've somehow learned to disagree, fight, clear the air, and get on with their lives. But some brothers and sisters feel a slow burn of rage and frustration toward each other. Even between fights they aren't at peace. The toll of long-term fury may prompt these siblings, to ice each other out rather than risk getting burned. A cold war seems better to them than either a hot war or the effort required to compromise and bury the hatchet.

At times the sibling cold war is a protective measure. Cutting off communication with a brother or sister may be a way to declare "time out" from the relationship—to cool off, settle down, and heal wounds. Under these circumstances, the cold war allows both parties a chance to avoid the damage they might sustain if they insisted on staying in touch. Jenny, for example, felt growing hostility toward her brother because she couldn't tolerate his harsh manner with his children. She broke off contact with him rather than risk an explosion that might end their relationship permanently.

At times, brothers and sisters are able to clear the air. However, it may be just a matter of time before hostilities resume. When a relationship is strained and volatile, one sibling may declare a cold war as a means of setting a limit to protect himself from a sibling's anger, ongoing disappointment, and pain.

Finally, there's the issue of how siblings do (or don't) communicate. Just as we learn other aspects of human interaction from our families, we learn how to express thoughts and feelings throughout childhood and adolescence. But what we learn depends greatly on what our parents say and do. In many families, communication is sporadic, confusing, unpredictable. Communication about anger and other "bad" feelings is especially awkward. One child's anger toward another may be discounted, mocked, even prohibited. In such situations it's understandably hard for sisters and brothers to know how to deal with the intensity and complexity of their own emotions, much less each other's. They never learned as children; they may still not know as adults.

Of these three factors, the most significant is probably faulty communication. These factors combine and intensify one anothers' effects, to be sure, but faulty communication between siblings may well be the detonator to these explosions. After all, even siblings with long-standing conflicts may succeed in resolving them if they can discuss their grievances and possible solutions. Even the most intense anger can diminish if brothers and sisters explain the sources of their rage and hear reassurances or offers of conciliation. But if communication skills are deficient or totally lacking, this is another matter altogether.

The fundamental cause of these cold wars is that siblings don't know how to talk about or even broach their feelings of hostility, rivalry, disappointment, envy, and anger toward each other. They know only their own emotions. Lacking a means of communication, all they can do with their anger is act it out. The great Prussian military strategist von Clausewitz once said, "War is diplomacy by other means"; sibling cold wars are communication by other means. Unfortunately, just as war is a miserable, destructive way to solve geopolitical problems, these cold wars are a miserable, destructive way to solve sibling problems. In many cases they don't solve problems at all and, in fact, may create more problems in the long run. And they create their own kinds of casualties—among not only brothers and sisters but others.

Here's the central issue. Feelings are so powerful a means of expression that they easily get out of hand. It's all too easy to express feelings as behavior—for instance, expressing anger as physical aggression. But if you can put your feelings into words, you're less likely to express them through inappropriate actions. Everyone experiences a repertoire of "negative" emotions—anger, hurt, guilt, anxiety, disappointment, frustration, and so forth. We all need to have these feelings understood. Unfortunately, when we're ill-equipped to give our emotional experiences a verbal form, the only recourse is raw behavior. Behavior becomes the vehicle that brothers and sisters use to let each other know they're enraged. One of the most common such behaviors is rejection. This is the most frequent source of sibling cold wars.

However, the general causes of these conflicts I've suggested aren't the only ones. Certain issues stemming from the clash between differing Good-Enough Sibling ideals serve as "flash points" that trigger a sibling cold war: expectations about unconditional emotional availability, tangible help (money, use of belongings, a place to stay—especially during times of crisis, such as when a sibling divorces or a parent dies), and various experiences of rejection.

These issues provide an incident, excuse, or misunderstanding that creates a focal point for old habits of conflict, resentment, or faulty communication. A brother takes offense at his sister's requests, claims, or comments. A sister feels insulted by her brother's behavior or lack of attention. A brother feels slighted or ignored by his brother's preoccupation with his wife or friends. A sister finds her sister too emotional, too unemotional, too attentive, or not attentive enough. The first misunderstanding leads to another, the second to a third, the third to a fourth, the fourth to an attack.

What sort of attack? Sometimes attacks are direct, active expressions of hostility—criticism, mockery, or even physical abuse. More often, however, they are indirect and passive: rejection rather than assault. These rejecting behaviors can take many shapes, but the most common are refusal to communicate (whether by conversation, phone calls, or letters), refusal or nonacknowledgment of gifts or "peace offerings," physical rejection (glaring, walking away, or other behaviors suggesting that the sibling doesn't exist), refusal to acknowledge a sibling's problem (physical or emotional pain or hardship), and hostile criticism or mockery of one sibling to other siblings, parents, or others.

Declaring a Truce, Negotiating a Treaty

Some combatants in sibling cold wars believe that the only way to deal with these battles is to become immune to the hurt or hostility they feel. This is an understandable reaction. It's hard to face months or even years of disapproval and rejection; it's just as hard to ease up if you're the one who started the hostilities and now feel a need to offer the olive branch. But allowing yourself to freeze is not a sensible response to the chill of a sibling cold war. You can take constructive rather than destructive action. Specifically, you can learn to become adaptive and more assertive in solving the fundamental causes of these conflicts.

Faulty communication skills are the major factor leading to sibling cold wars. If you have no way of discussing disagreements and the emotions they engender, you're more likely to stonewall your brothers and sisters. When the cold war is in progress, you're all the more helpless if you want to call a truce or negotiate a treaty. So what's the solution?

As with so many complex problems, there's no easy answer, but there is a starting point: simply improving your communication skills.

Improving your communication skills is, first and foremost, a question of being *open*. This sounds self-evident, but it's a point that all too often gets lost in the shuffle. You must be open to your own feelings; you must also leave yourself open to your sibling's feelings. *You must talk to each other.*

This means different things depending on which side of the battle line you're on. Are you the sibling who feels rejected? Or are you the sibling who's done the rejecting?

If You Feel Rejected

If you're the sibling who feels rejected, being open means swallowing your pride and expressing your emotions about the conflict. This is a gamble. You may end up rejected yet again. But it's a gamble well worth taking, especially if you can state your case without accusation or bitterness. Perhaps your sister or brother will follow your lead and reciprocate; perhaps not. At the least you will be able to stop walking around swamped with terrible feelings. If your brother or sister has cut you off, at least you can address your feelings; this in turn starts moving you out of an amputated state. If you can express your feelings and learn to avoid provocative, antagonistic remarks, your brother or sister may even relate to your words enough to move beyond his or her own disruptive behavior.

For instance, Maria's mother needs more and more assistance as she grows older. Maria, who is her mother's primary caregiver, wants to be helpful but feels overwhelmed. To ease the burden, she recently asked her sister, Stephanie, to check in with her now and then about their mother's situation. Stephanie neglected to call for several weeks. Maria thought about nudging her but didn't—she felt it shouldn't be necessary. When Stephanie's silence continued, Maria decided to cut off communication.

Maria has been a patient of mine for some months now, and we recently tackled the issue of her cold war with Stephanie. Maria's most immediate task was to make her feelings known to her sister plainly but without accusation or anger. After working on this issue awhile, Maria managed to tell Stephanie, "Look, I understand that you're busy, but this is our mother we're talking about. She needs us. I feel emotionally drained looking after her alone. I don't expect you to do very much—just call me from time to time to hear me out. I need your support." Eventually Stephanie got the message and was able to respond. The response wasn't as frequent as Maria would have liked, but at least Stephanie tried. Maria herself made great strides in dealing with the tendency to declare war whenever she felt offended; she didn't attack Stephanie but instead focused on explaining what she needed from her. Meanwhile, Maria is now dealing with a broader issue: the disparity between who she wants her sister to be and who she really is.

If You've Done the Rejecting

If you're the sibling who's done the rejecting, you need to look at the nature and intensity of your anger and ask yourself what your priorities are. Is expressing your anger most important—even at the expense of severing your sibling bond? Or is your priority to change the relationship, to have a stronger sense of siblinghood? Perhaps you have real grievances. Fine. But is declaring yourself the wronged party more important than sorting through the issues and finding common ground? Perhaps you get angry because you feel your sibling won't understand. But if you can't talk about the situation, your brother or sister will never have a chance to understand at all.

Note that the core issue for each kind of communication is anger. How do you deal with your anger? For many sisters and brothers, so many small wounds have accumulated that they feel like a terrible gash. The level of rage they experience is very difficult to contain. All they know is that they're *right*. One of the tasks for siblings on either side of the battle line is therefore to decide what matters more: to be right, or to have a relationship with a sister or brother.

No matter which side you're on, what course of action should you take? That depends. You'll have to evaluate your own situation and decide what's most likely to work out.

If you can manage the presence of mind, make a phone call and say, "Look, this has gone on between us long enough. I've been very angry with you, but maybe it's time for us to put our differences aside." Put your anger in statements, not in accusations or threats: "I was very upset by what happened, but now I'd like for us to get together and talk things over."

If, however, you feel that talking about your anger will lead to further rage and a loss of control, I suggest that you write a letter. This can be just as helpful as a conversation in person. It allows you to state your case calmly; it even allows you to think it through more carefully.

In both instances, there's no guarantee about what will come of your effort. Still, it's worth a try. Whatever else, this open expression will bring the issues into focus in your own mind—no small achievement.

Here's an example that illustrates most of the issues we've been discussing. Bob and Arlene are husband and wife. Bob and his sister, Brynne, have had a complex and mutually uneasy relationship for many years. For instance, Bob asked to borrow some of his sister's luggage. Brynne refused, saying, "I may want to use it, so you'll have to get your own." Bob felt so insulted by this response that he cut off all communication with his sister. They haven't talked in six years.

Arlene now wants her husband to make amends with Brynne. Bob was reluctant initially; then he consented. Better to set aside his anger, he thought. Better to work toward a truce. So Bob called Brynne and said, "My feelings were really hurt by what you did—I was furious when you wouldn't loan me the luggage. But can't we sort things out?" To Bob's surprise, Brynne didn't seem to recall the incident— or, worse yet, she *acted* as if she didn't recall it. "I don't remember that. Let me give it some thought and I'll get back to you," she said. Bob didn't press the issue. Maybe Brynne's response was a way of buying time to think things over. If so, fine. Bob waited for a further chance to talk with his sister.

Brynne never called back.

Was Bob's call an exercise in futility? On the contrary—despite a less-than-ideal resolution, the effort paid off by clarifying Bob's thinking and easing his pent-up rage.

At first, Bob felt the temptation to revert to his earlier anger at Brynne. He'd reject her altogether! However, I presented two options to Bob in therapy. Either he could continue the cold war, with the risk of side effects from his bottled-up anger—side effects that might harm his marriage, his work, or his health—or he could look at his sister with new eyes. Brynne is Brynne: no more, no less. Brynne isn't the Good-Enough Sibling that Bob has always wanted her to be. Brynne wasn't considerate or caring six years ago; she still isn't. Nevertheless, does Brynne's lack of certain capacities for involvement mean that Bob should sever *all ties* with her? Or does it make more sense for Bob to modify the ways he views Brynne and protect himself by avoiding unrealistic expectations of his sister?

Bob now feels relatively at peace with the situation. He still wishes

Brynne could be more responsive and considerate. Yet he's learned to see that she isn't, and that there's no point in pretending that she is. By setting aside his anger at Brynne, Bob has moved beyond the cold war—he has thawed out of the deep chill the conflict cast over him—and he can now focus more energy on his relationships with his wife, his children, and his friends.

8

The Invisible Sibling

Sibling cold wars are most significant for the damage they often do to brothers and sisters themselves. As a result of them, what may have been a difficult relationship can collapse into ruinous silence. Yet what makes these cold wars even more heartbreaking is that they don't damage just the principal combatants. They can hurt other people as well—people whom either or both siblings may love and value; people the siblings have no intention or awareness of hurting. Ignoring the occurrence of a sibling cold war may affect your spouse, your children, your friends, even employers, co-workers, or total strangers. For the cold war is often far more powerful and extensive than it seems. Neglecting the issues that create cold wars will not make them go away; on the contrary, neglect merely displaces those issues onto other relationships.

Unfortunately, even the greatest geographic distances, the thickest walls, the deepest silence can't keep your sibling out of your life. Your brother or sister will still be present on some level. This level may be psychological rather than physical, but it's powerful all the same. As in so many other ways, "out of sight" does not mean "out of mind." The conflict between you and your brother or sister will haunt you till you make some effort to acknowledge and understand it.

Conflict seeks resolution. Bad feelings seek relief. Whether consciously or unconsciously, people try to remedy their hurts, heal their wounds, and repair the damages inflicted on them by sibling conflict. This drive toward resolution most often happens by means of what I call the Invisible Sibling.

The Invisible Sibling appears in many forms and turns up in many situations. He can appear at home disguised as a husband or a son. She can show up at the workplace in the form of an employer or a colleague. He can turn up as an uncle, a nephew, or a brother-in-law. She can arrive in the image of a friend, an acquaintance, or a total stranger. In many cases Invisible Siblings appear precisely when and where you least expect them.

The Invisible Sibling is simply someone *other* than a sibling whose presence in your life evokes old feelings of siblinghood, some of which may be positive (love, appreciation, admiration) and some negative (dislike, hatred, contempt). He can appear when you feel wounded by an injustice that your brother has committed against you; she can appear when you relinquish your role as a Supersibling and disengage from a manipulative or demanding sister; he can appear when you have a fundamentally positive relationship with your brother or sister that nonetheless includes "unfinished business." In short, the Invisible Sibling is a means by which you attempt to deal with the legacies of your sibling relationships—legacies that may be either positive or negative, including sibling rivalry.

The Invisible Sibling can be either a creative or a destructive force. Abby provides a perfect instance of the creativity possible in dealing with Invisible Sibling issues; by contrast, Eric illustrates the potential frustration inherent in these issues.

Years of hard work and careful planning had finally brought Abby to the goal she'd always sought: art director of the children's book division in a large publishing company. It was the field she loved and the best possible position for her interests. She didn't doubt that she'd thrive there for years.

The only problem was Abby's boss. Maggie was the publisher who oversaw not only Abby's division, but several others as well. No one argued that Maggie wasn't good at her job; she encouraged and in fact demanded excellence in every aspect of book production. But her managerial style gave pause to even her most enthusiastic supporters. The kindest nickname that Abby ever heard for her boss was Dragon Lady.

Abby found herself ambivalent about Maggie from the start. On the one hand, she admired this woman's commitment to excellence; on the other hand, she dreaded disagreeing with her. And Abby wasn't one to be pushed around. She'd had enough of that from her sister, June—someone for whom (as Abby herself put it) bossiness was its own reward. Abby had suffered June's dominance long enough that she had a short temper with anyone who pulled similar stunts; since June had rejected all efforts to settle their differences as adults, Abby had come to feel depleted when dealing with *anyone* who treated her as less than an equal. So it didn't surprise Abby when she felt uneasy around her new boss. Maggie reminded her all too much of June.

After some initial fights, however, Abby made a discovery. Maggie *did* remind Abby of her sister. Maggie *was* bossy. Yet there was something else at work. Maggie demanded a lot from Abby, but she also provided the material resources to accomplish what she demanded; and Maggie expressed her appreciation of what Abby accomplished both in what she said and how she behaved. Maggie was bossy, but she also provided genuine leadership and—even more surprising— inspiration. As Abby got to know Maggie better, she came to see her as a genuine role model. More than that: She came to see Maggie as a kind of big sister who spoke with authority because she actually *knew* more—the sister, in fact, that Abby had always wanted.

When Eric returned to college for his senior year, he moved with two other students into a house off campus. The arrangement seemed perfect: the right balance between proximity to classes and distance from the commotion of undergraduate life. It was Eric's first place of his own. The fact that he'd be sharing it didn't seem a problem. Anything would have been preferable to living at home, which Eric had found financially convenient during his first three years in college but stressful otherwise—especially because of Eric's difficult relationship with his younger brother.

Eric and Sam had never gotten along. Sam acted like a dictator, ordering his brothers around. The boys' parents didn't approve of their last-born son's dominating behavior, but he was, after all, the baby of the family. They'd always given him his way; he was so strong-willed that it seemed easier to relent, so Eric and his older brother put up with Sam for lack of a clear alternative. A series of arguments between Eric and Sam had grown increasingly violent, however, and Eric had packed his bags, stormed out of the family home, and cut off all communication with that spoiled little brat. Now, Eric felt he'd finally got his neck out from under Sam's boot.

He soon ran into a source of unexpected trouble, though. One of Eric's new housemates—an acquaintance named Jerry—had convinced his best pal, Dean, to rent the place too. Although Eric didn't know Jerry well, he could see that Jerry wasn't the problem. Dean, however, was another matter. He acted as if he knew everything and could do anything. Eric tried to appease him at first but without success. Kidding Dean out of his pretensions didn't work either—the guy was devoid of humor. Within a few weeks, Eric and Dean were exchanging taunts and insults; soon they could scarcely tolerate each other's presence; at one point they almost came to blows. After less than two months, Eric moved out in a huff. He wasn't going to tolerate this sort of treatment. If he'd wanted to battle with someone, he could have stayed home and continued fighting with his brother.

These two stories suggest how the Invisible Sibling can lead to the closeness and growth we seek in relationships; alternatively, the Invisible Sibling can lead to further difficulties and frustrations. The Invisible Sibling can become a way of resolving certain otherwise insoluble problems in your sibling relationships. However, if you are unaware of the power inherent in him, or her, the Invisible Sibling can have explosive consequences for you life.

Alison is the oldest of four grown sisters. These women have been in conflict with one another since childhood, with each competing intensely for their distant mother's attentions. In their household, no one gained anything without someone else losing—or at least that was how the girls perceived the situation.

Some years ago, Alison had invited her youngest sister, Jodie, to stay at her house. Jodie didn't really want to stay, so she moved out. But when she moved, Jodie lied to their mother, telling her that Alison had thrown her out. Their mother never forgave Alison for her supposed heartlessness. Jodie later disrupted relationships between Alison and her other sisters. Alison called Jodie a liar. Understandably, she was furious about Jodie's behavior, but she did nothing to confront her. Instead, she waged a cold war and refused to have anything to do with Jodie.

Enter the Invisible Sibling! Alison now lives with her new husband, Scott, and Scott's teenage son by his first marriage. Recently, Alison has started having severe conflicts with her stepson, Russell. Alison describes Russell exactly as she describes her sister: "He's a liar—always making trouble." Stepmother and stepson just can't get along. Alison's marriage started to hit the rocks when she gave Scott an ultimatum: "I can't tolerate that kid in my house any longer. It's either the boy or me."

According to Alison, Russell is destroying their marriage by coming between Alison and Scott. In fact, Russell—though much younger than Jodie and of the opposite sex—is Alison's Invisible Sibling. Alison has replicated her past sibling battles in her new family; her stepson evokes the competitiveness she once felt toward her sisters as she battles for the resource of her husband's attention. Russell is the lightning rod that Alison will strike with bolts of the rage she feels toward Jodie.

During a therapy session not long ago, I told Alison, "So by throwing Russell out you're finally going to get back at your sister. You're going to get to throw her out at last."

She looked at me in surprise, then said, "I guess you could put it that way."

I said, "The only problem is, you're going to wreck your marriage, too."

Alison said, "At this point I don't care if I do. I can't stand Russell." She grew angrier and angrier.

When she calmed down, however, Alison was able to understand the dynamics of the Invisible Sibling at work in her life. We could then begin dealing with her unresolved feelings toward Jodie so that she could grasp the impact that this old conflict had on her. This new perspective enabled her to let go of the ultimatum she'd given her husband; she worked things out in a far more constructive way with her spouse and stepson.

Another patient of mine, Stuart, is the youngest of seven siblings—one sister and six brothers. The children's father died when Stuart was still a boy. Stuart's mother felt constantly overwhelmed, and the children vied for the limited resources of maternal time, energy, and attention. In addition, one brother in particular was a bully who had received carte blanche from their mother to control the family. Stuart felt enraged with both his mother and his brother over this situation.

Now well into adulthood, Stuart finds that he has difficulty getting along with people. He often ends up being thrown out of groups. Stuart tries to be cooperative—a "team player"—but he invariably develops competitive feelings toward someone in his immediate surroundings. Toward whom? Usually Stuart's Invisible Sibling is whomever he happens to be working with. Because he never feels sufficiently powerful compared with other people, and because he fears losing out on his share of the "goods," Stuart compensates by being aggressive and constantly putting his integrity on the line. He can't pass up a chance to tell people that he's better, stronger, brighter, funnier, and more competent than they.

As a result, Stuart constantly goes up against his "invisible" brother; no matter where he turns, Stuart ends up in conflict. Since he won't face up to his *real* brother, he ends up fighting with the Invisible Sibling, who takes any number of shapes and forms.

Making the Invisible Sibling Visible

The Invisible Sibling is an effort to remedy scarred sibling relationships. The most important thing to realize, however, is that you probably have no idea that the hurt caused by your sibling relationship could be forcefully affecting another important relationship in your life. That is, you have no idea that you're dealing with an Invisible Sibling. This is the most problematic aspect of the Invisible Sibling: that it's invisible. You don't see any sibling conflict either because you stopped dealing with your sister or brother directly or because you've cut back considerably on your involvement with her or him. All you're aware of is that you're having real problems with some other significant person in your life—your wife, your boss, your friend. In a sense you're boxing with shadows—or ghosts. The difficulty is that, although your interpersonal problems are legitimate, the presence of the Invisible Sibling is intensifying them. These marital, professional, or personal conflicts are real and need to be resolved, yet you're less likely to get a handle on them if you can't separate out your unresolved sibling issues. Therefore, the most important task before you is to make the Invisible Sibling visible. Only then can you acquire the knowledge of what you're dealing with—knowledge that will help you decide on an appropriate response.

The first step is to consider that if you're engaging in a conflict with one person in particular, some of that conflict may have roots in your relationship with a sister or brother. This realization alone won't solve the conflict, but it's a necessary start: it gives you a frame of reference that offers clues to the nature of the problem you're experiencing. This will provide a critical sense of perspective and objectivity. Otherwise you're left wrestling with a mass of chaotic feelings and no means of taking hold of them. Once you begin to identify the problem as an Invisible Sibling issue, however, you start to redefine the situation.

Diana's circumstances show how this process of redefinition works. For many years, Diana has dealt with a frustrating co-worker, Jill. "Jill has mastered the art of putting down people by comparing herself to them," Diana explains. "She says, 'Well, you don't have a husband, so you wouldn't understand.' Or 'You've never had kids, so you wouldn't know.' " Jill's put-downs have exasperated Diana to the point of distraction. But recently Diana reached an insight that clarified her feelings about Jill. In conversation with a friend, she realized that Jill's condescending behavior reminded Diana of her sister, Marge: "I figured out that this is exactly what my sister would do—and still does. And Jill reminds me very much of my sister. So I can deal with her put-downs now. I still can't deal with my sister directly, but I've learned to step back from Jill."

The next step in dealing with an Invisible Sibling is to consider what went wrong between you and your brother or sister. Why do you feel misunderstood, unappreciated, or hurt? Look at the source of your anger or resentment to get as clear a picture as possible of what specifically you found objectionable in the relationship. Then begin to look at your relationship with that other person to see if your conflict revolves around a similar issue. In the previous instance, Diana realized that Jill was behaving in a manner similiar to how her sister treated her. You can start to see how you may be viewing other people as if they were your sister or brother. This insight provides you with the means to deal more objectively and realistically with your immediate conflict.

The Invisible Sibling becomes the recipient of many feelings derived from your relationships with brothers and sisters. These feelings may be conscious, but often they aren't. You may be aware that this or that person reminds you of your brother, for instance, but it's just as likely that the connection is subtle; it's also likely that, even if you recognize it, you miss the magnitude of its implications.

Begin by considering the following three circumstances that can give rise to the Invisible Sibling.

First, the Invisible Sibling may appear if you feel that your sister or brother has done you an injustice—has wronged, cheated, manipulated, belittled, humiliated, controlled, or refused to acknowledge you. For instance, Nancy looked out for her younger sister, Cindy, since childhood, yet Cindy was never appreciative of Nancy. On the contrary, Cindy ignored and rebuffed her sister's numerous efforts and talked about Nancy behind her back with both family members and friends. Nancy has struggled for a long time with her resentment of Cindy's response. Recently, she has felt a similar resentment toward a co-worker named Pam. Nancy brought Pam into the company years ago and, as her mentor, shared with Pam everything she knew about the business. Pam, however, never acknowledged Nancy's help and went behind her back with the boss to get a better job for herself. She bad-mouthed Nancy just as Cindy had done to get what she wanted.

Second, the Invisible Sibling may appear if your relationship with a brother or sister changes and you feel a sense of loss. For instance, Randy had always looked up to her older sister Carrie. Carrie was bright, beautiful, popular, and gifted in many ways. Yet Carrie never quite pulled her life together: She achieved none of her personal or professional goals and blamed others for her lack of success. Randy felt disappointed that her role model had let her down. As a result, she sought out seemingly high-powered women as business partners. Unfortunately, these women often disappointed her, since they seldom attained their goals either.

Third, the Invisible Sibling may appear if you need to heal unresolved sibling rivalry. Amy is a good example of this situation. Two years older than Pete, Amy had always felt intense rivalry toward her brother. She expressed this rivalry most often by trying to exercise power over him in whatever ways she could. For the most part, she did so successfully. Yet she felt guilt and remorse over her manipulative behavior. As an adult, Amy has been drawn to men she could look after, especially on the job, as if to "make up" for what she had done to her brother.

In each of these instances, the reason for the Invisible Sibling's appearance is essentially the same. It is a vehicle by which people can both become the sister or brother they want to be and have the sister or brother they feel they didn't have. The Invisible Sibling is therefore a way for people to pursue their ideal of the Good-Enough Sibling. For instance, trying to help Pam was a way for Nancy to pursue being a Good-Enough Sibling in the hope of reaching a better outcome than she had with her sister.

The Invisible Sibling on the Job

Leslie has almost unceasing conflicts at work. She feels that her boss doesn't recognize her skills and undermines her efforts. She also feels that her colleagues lie to her, conspire against her, and generally try to harm her professionally. Leslie finds the workplace a constant web of injustices and humiliations.

However, the source of her problem isn't professional competition at all but rather her own childhood. Through several months of psychotherapy, Leslie has recalled a powerful experience that took place when she was seven years old. She was playing outside when her sister and brother broke a vase inside the house. Leslie ran in to see what had made the noise. Her siblings fled out the back door just as their father discovered the wreckage. "What have you done!" he shouted. Leslie protested: "I wasn't even here! *They* did it!" But her brother and sister ganged up against Leslie. Her father didn't support her, so Leslie felt unjustly blamed. She has carried the emotional scar of this incident for decades. Now it comes up at work. Never mind the reality of the workplace; Leslie is constantly battling her siblings and father as they appear as her Invisible Siblings.

If you feel angry, resentful, and wronged at work, you may well be dealing with the Invisible Sibling. It's possible, of course, that you face real injustices or personality clashes on the job; there's no shortage of discrimination, bias, and abuse in the work realm. But these two possibilities aren't mutually exclusive. Genuine work conflicts may be intensified and distorted by Invisible Sibling issues. Whatever else, you should consider the presence of the Invisible Sibling before you attribute your work problems solely to external sources.

Start by asking yourself these questions:

- Have you experienced feelings of anger, resentment, and being mistreated only at your current job?

- Or have frustrating work situations caused you problems before, perhaps even repeatedly?

- Do you look to employers or co-workers for constant support, encouragment, and consistency—only to find yourself feeling disappointed time after time?

These questions concern the pattern of your emotional response to work situations. A yes answer to any of them suggests the possibility that at least some of your difficulties are not so much *caused by* people at work as they are *focused on* them. The more yes answers you've given, the more likely it is that you bring your own script to the job and generate some of the difficulties. That is not to say that the people you're working with aren't problematic. But your response to them may be heightening the conflict. If you look more closely at the situation, you'll probably see that you are replicating your sibling relationship. The more consistently you have experienced these feelings in different work settings, the more likely it is that your conflicts suggest the presence of an Invisible Sibling.

Another indicator of the Invisible Sibling is intensity of feeling. If your feelings about work-related problems are so consuming that they disrupt your other activities or overall emotional stability, then factors other than professional issues may be affecting you. Again, this statement doesn't imply that work-related issues aren't present or genuinely difficult—only that unresolved sibling rivalry may be complicating them.

The Invisible Sibling in Personal Life

How do you know if you're dealing with an Invisible Sibling in a personal relationship? Again, the answers to certain key questions may tip you off:

- Are you angry at your spouse, lover, or friends for seemingly petty reasons?

- Or, if your anger about personal conflicts seems justified, does it seem conspicuously out of proportion to the conflicts themselves?

- Are you feeling guilty without clear cause, or guilty out of proportion to whatever real issue may be causing the guilt?

- Are you feeling other emotions (resentment, hurt, jealousy, and so on) without cause or out of proportion to the cause?

A yes answer to one or more of these questions suggests the presence of old sibling rivalry issues.

For example, Tina has been in conflict with her sister Lori for many years because Tina always feels controlled by Lori. Now the sisters rarely talk. One weekend, Tina and her close friend Lilith had planned a typical Saturday of dancing—something that the sisters used to do together as well. Then Tina made plans with another friend for Friday night, simply because she got an unexpected invitation. Lilith learned of Tina's Friday plans and snapped that Tina should make sure she didn't spend all her money and energy before Saturday. Tina was furious at Lilith for telling her what to do. After a series of arguments and misunderstandings, she ended up canceling both sets of plans and spent the whole weekend alone.

Tina had vented a lot of the smoldering anger that she feels toward her sister at her friend instead. She had cut off the relationship with Lori because she could not stand up to her sister's control. Yet here she was, fighting with her closest friend over the exact same behavior that had precipitated a fight with her sister. Lilith's behavior was the same as Lori's—and it drew the same response from Tina. However, in other instances, Tina has experienced Lilith as behaving like her sister when in fact Lilith's behavior was not the same at all. Tina is so consumed by negative feelings toward Lori that these feelings cloud her vision and prompt her to see everyone's behavior as controlling even when it's not.

This story suggests another aspect of the Invisible Sibling. Often, the greatest indicator of Invisible Sibling problems is a break in the sibling relationship. Unresolved anger and hurt lead to an abrupt severing of the sibling tie. Then sibling issues are rerouted into Invisible Sibling relationships as a means of working them through. What is the implication? For most people, there's no end to a relationship even after they say good-bye. Despite telling your sister, "I'm never going to talk with you again," you're almost certain to continue at some point. The conversation may not be direct, but it will occur. Unfortunately, the indirect nature of this conversation—with the Invisible Sibling rather than with your real sibling—will make it all the more difficult for you to recognize what's happening.

What's going on in all these situations? What explains the way that the Invisible Sibling pops up in strange places and at unexpected times?

The phenomenon at work is displacement. Displacement is an unconscious psychological defense mechanism that is employed to transfer emotions toward a different person or situation. Angry, hostile, and resentful feelings are commonly displaced toward a safer and less threatening person or situation. With the Invisible Sibling, you are unconsciously taking the emotions from your sibling relationship and displacing them onto another person in your life.

If you are furious with your brother or feeling wronged by your sister's actions, and if you do not resolve these feelings directly with your sibling, it's probable that through displacement you will continue to experience the feelings you have about your sister or brother about someone else.

Making Sense, Taking Control

Let's say that you've detected an Invisible Sibling and made him or her visible. You now recognize that you've been fighting with your boss because of an unresolved conflict with your brother. Or you see that you're fighting with your wife because of old resentments toward your sister. These insights are valuable in helping you locate the source of the conflict with an Invisible Sibling. Now you must decide what to do.

Before proceeding, however, let's consider a question that many people ask when dealing with these situations. Why dredge up all the old feelings about your brothers and sisters? Can't you leave well enough alone? Sometimes you can—and should. But often this just isn't possible. In many cases the urge to avoid will complicate rather than simplify your situation.

The Invisible Sibling is a powerful and persistent force. Ignored in one form, he or she will reappear in another. Let's say you're arguing with your boss. You begin to realize that he reminds you of your brother. If you avoid dealing with the similarity of feelings, the problem will prevail. Let's say you quit your job. So much for *that* boss, you say with a sigh of relief. But what about your next employer? Will you feel surprised if he, too, ends up bearing a striking resemblance to your domineering brother?

Because of the fundamental push that all people experience toward making things better, you crave a deeper, more substantial resolution to your conflict. This longing is likely to perpetuate additional Invisible Siblings in the hope that you'll find the kind of sibling relationship you desire. For this reason, it's compelling to deal with the feelings generated by the Invisible Sibling. You can proceed by determining whether you need to confront your sister or brother directly with the feelings you have. First, however, you must decide what you hope to accomplish.

Do you want simply to vent your anger at your sister or brother without concern for what the response may be? Or are you hoping in some way to change your relationship?

If your hope is to alter your relationship, the next question to consider is whether your brother or sister will be able to respond constructively to your feelings. He or she may get so angry that the conflict will escalate rather than reach resolution. You need to try to determine whether both of you will be able to handle constructively the powerful feelings you want to discuss. You may sense that your sibling can't deal with this kind of emotional conversation. You may consequently decide not to approach him or her at all. This decision will help you decide what your next step should be.

Essentially you are trying to figure out the best way to address whatever has been troubling you. This may mean talking with your sibling or it may mean confronting the situation within yourself. Either way, making sense and taking control requires recognizing that the Invisible Sibling is present, then addressing the issues in the proper forum. If you decide not to confront your sibling with your feelings, perhaps you can work them through in terms of the conflict in your Invisible Sibling relationship.

The key is to figure out what you are feeling, as well as what the origins of these emotions may be. That is, you need to look for the roots of your anger and resentment. Whether through psychotherapy, dialogue in your family, or introspection, you must trace the conflict to its source.

Recognizing that you have a lot of emotions—feeling blamed, faulted, rejected, or whatever—can let you put them in their proper place rather than displace them onto other relationships. Once you confront what you have experienced with your sisters and brothers and acknowledge its powerful impact, you'll be able to handle yourself better in your relationships with others.

If you can recognize that you're dealing with an Invisible Sibling scenario, you may realize that you're seeing events through the eyes of a child—a child whose chief "colleagues" for many years were siblings—and that what you're seeing is partially distorted by your child-eyed perceptions. Specifically, your view of your brothers or sisters influences the present picture. Your new, clearer perception may provide you with a broader vision—one that allows you to see co-workers in their own right rather than in the light of siblinghood. This vision may also allow you to approach these people more openly, less guardedly. This new perspective can help you in two ways: first, it frees you to act more clear-sightedly in the present; second, it frees you to come to terms with certain aspects of your past.

Dealing with Invisible Sibling issues is a path toward personal growth. In fact, the Invisible Sibling is often a powerful and constructive force for resolving grievances about long-past sibling rivalries. The Invisible Sibling can be a creative, healing force when you form a relationship with a spouse, friend, friend, boss, or co-worker who is receptive to you and values you as a person. Under these circumstances, the Invisible Sibling provides a means toward growth and change, especially when the connection has been cut between you and a sibling with whom you have deep misunderstandings or with whom you were never close.

The Invisible Sibling may also allow you to say to a friend or colleague the words that you weren't able to say to a brother or sister. Alternatively, the Invisible Sibling may foster insights into the reality of your brother or sister—that is, into what he or she *is* rather than what you wish him or her to be. The Invisible Sibling provides the forum for cultivating and sustaining quality sibling relationships with people other than our own kin. It's not by accident that we speak of a boss who is "just like a big sister" or of friends who are "like brothers to me." Brotherhood and sisterhood are too valuable to confine to our biological siblings.

9

Cross Fire and Fallout

———

Another arena in which sibling rivalry can fester is the relationships that brothers and sisters have with their other relatives. All the emotions that attend sibling rivalry—competition, envy, jealousy, resentment, and so forth—can come into play in these relationships. Sometimes, as a legacy of such rivalry, one sibling may express these feelings by comparing his or her children with those of brothers and sisters. By this means, children often become unwitting pawns in their parents' unresolved conflicts with their own siblings.

The result is what I call cross fire and fallout: the side effects of sibling conflicts that can wound "innocent bystanders" as well as siblings themselves. Cross fire and fallout all too frequently result when brothers or sisters are unable or unwilling to see the nature of their misunderstandings. Their parents, other siblings, spouses, and especially children—that is, the siblings' nieces and nephews—are all potential victims of incidents triggered by old feelings of sibling rivalry.

The Hidden Significance of Uncles and Aunts, Nephews and Nieces

Nephews and nieces often present their uncles and aunts with an unexpected link to their siblings. If one of your siblings has children, you may suddenly find yourself thrust into the adjunct role of aunt or uncle. This realm contains factors that extend from the sibling relationship. Rivalry can continue to be played out through issues of control, such as sharing the kids, making continued demands for baby-sitting, and so forth. Libby's brother Ken, for instance, wouldn't think twice about calling her on short notice and assuming that she would come over to baby-sit for Ken's little boy. Whenever Libby protested that she had other plans, Ken would counteract her with his "after all I've done for you" line. Libby ended up feeling forced into her responsibilities as an aunt: held hostage by her brother.

Futhermore, being an uncle or aunt may become an extension of your identity as a Good-Enough Sibling. I often see patients whose sense of themselves as Good-Enough Siblings has become directly linked to the way they function in their roles as aunt or uncle. In instances when parents may be having emotional or financial difficulties, uncles and aunts may serve as assistant parents or even—in extreme cases—as legally adoptive parents. So the role of aunt or uncle may have powerful effects on how you see yourself and your commitments to your family.

What potential is inherent in our aunt/uncle–niece/nephew relationships? For many people, this relationship may serve to address old sibling issues and become either positive or negative in its own right. Brothers and sisters sometimes let us down, or we let them down; our needs and abilities are out of sync; we conflict over values; we ache from misunderstandings both old and new. These shortcomings disappoint us even if they cease to surprise us.

When your sibling relationship doesn't fulfill your expectations, you're usually left with a sense of deprivation. One way of redressing this deprivation is to shift your attentions to someone similar or close to your sister or brother. Nephews and nieces are understandable and often convenient recipients for this shift. In this way, nieces and nephews can become Invisible Siblings. Being an aunt or uncle allows you to express concern and affection toward your nieces or nephews in ways similar to what you might like to use with your siblings. Uncle/aunt–nephew/niece relationships are in this sense a way to actualize your notion of yourself as a Good-Enough Sibling. They are a forum for transforming your ideals about siblinghood into reality. They give you a legitimate way to fulfill yourself.

In her own family, Yvonne often found herself in the rôles of Helper, Counselor, Nurse, and, in many ways, Supersibling. She resented these roles more and more deeply over the years. She battled with her older brother constantly over his pushing her into so many family responsibilities. When he married and his wife had a child, Yvonne was delighted but determined not to let him exploit her as a glorified baby-sitter for her nephew.

To her surprise, however, Yvonne established an intensely close bond with her nephew, Taylor. She found this little boy more insightful (and in some ways more mature) than his troubled parents; Taylor in turn found Yvonne a source of stability that he would have lacked otherwise. As Taylor grows up, he and his aunt will become closer. Yvonne even finds that this relationship has brought her closer to her brother.

Such a positive uncle/aunt–nephew/niece relationship can be rewarding to all parties while serving as an opportunity for healing a damaged sibling bond.

Alternatively, such a relationship can be negative or strained. This can occur for several reasons.

Sometimes a niece or nephew ends up serving as an outlet or lightning rod for anger toward a brother or sister and becomes an Invisible Sibling. This phenomenon introduces the problem inherent in the Invisible Sibling: losing track of both your anger and its origins. Venting rage against your niece won't help you if it's your sister who has enraged you. Needless to say, it doesn't do your niece much good either. An aunt/uncle–niece/nephew relationship may also be problematic if it becomes a forum for a continuation of sibling rivalry. There are emotional risks for both parties if your niece or nephew is less significant to you than is the child's connection to your sibling. Your niece or nephew may become merely a stand-in for the alienated sister or brother. This sort of arrangement seems unfair to everyone—most of all the child. It's as if the conflicts of one generation are being visited upon the next.

For example, Luís never got along well with his younger brother,

Armando. He felt that Armando was his parents' favored child. Armando got all the opportunities: better schooling, more attention, more affection. By contrast, Luís felt ignored, even dismissed by his parents—forced to struggle for everything he accomplished and for every bit of praise his parents bestowed on him. In fact, Armando always seemed to get the lion's share of everything.

It was no surprise that, when Armando married and started a family, Luís resented the disparity between his brother's fortunes and his own. More than anything else, Luís envied Armando his relationships with his sons. And when he saw that Armando and his wife favored Miguel, their older son, over Jesse, their younger son, Luís could scarcely contain his exasperation. He resolved to redress the balance. When his brother came with his family for a visit, Luís showered attention on Jesse and gave a cold shoulder to Miguel. Miguel should taste rejection, Luís thought, as Luís himself had tasted it long ago. And Jesse should feel the warmth of someone's favor even if his parents passed him by. It was only proper. Not only would it do the boys good to have the tables turned but it also seemed a harmless way to get back at Armando.

Miguel hadn't done anything to warrant Luís's coolness; he was an innocent bystander caught in the brothers' cross fire. And Luís's lack of warmth toward a blameless fourteen-year-old did nothing to help him resolve his anger toward Armando.

Rachel, the middle of three sisters, faced an even more intricate situation. Rachel has had frequent problems getting along with her younger sister, Dolores, but few disagreements with the oldest, Beth. Each of the sisters has two children. Despite the conflicts between Rachel and Dolores, their children often play together and get along well. On one occasion, however, Rachel's kids told the others that Rachel couldn't stand Aunt Dolores. This message got back to Dolores, who was furious. Rachel stayed clear of the children's effort to sort through their mothers' conflicts; she felt that the kids were entitled to work things out on their own. But Rachel and Dolores haven't talked with each other for months. In some respects the nieces and nephews have ended up chasing out their aunts' conflicts.

Why do some nieces or nephews end up catching the "bullets" intended for siblings? At times the blood tie is sufficient explanation. That is, if you're mad at your sister, you'll express the anger toward your niece simply because she's your sister's daughter. It's a question of guilt by association. At other times, appearance can be a reason. If you're mad at your sister, you may displace your anger onto the one of her children who most resembles her mother. The actual reasons that trigger cross fire are unlimited, but what's most significant here is that the misdirected rage can hurt innocent parties. Often, the connection isn't clearly recognized. That is, you may not see that you're annoyed with your niece because she reminds you of your sister.

A more extreme instance of this situation is when nieces and nephews become bargaining chips for power between brothers and sisters. This phenomenon is a kind of fallout from sibling "cold wars," discussed in Chapter 7. Just as in divorce, siblings may end up engaged in a kind of "custody" battle over the children. The custody in question isn't a legal matter; however, it may evoke emotions just as intense as those arising when a marriage falls apart.

For example, a patient of mine named Marilyn fought long and hard with her sister, Ellen, over many issues, but their most bitter arguments concerned Ellen's preschool-aged daughter. Marilyn could tolerate "splitting up" with Ellen, but she couldn't imagine losing contact with her niece. Ellen, however, initially refused to allow Marilyn any time with the girl. This refusal prompted Marilyn to accuse her sister of emotional blackmail, heartless tactics, and lack of consideration not only for Marilyn but also for her daughter. Ellen now agrees to let Marilyn visit with her niece—but only if Ellen is there to supervise. Marilyn is furious at her sister's mistrustful and controlling behavior, and she feels insulted by these "terms of visitation."

If you're caught up in one of more of these situations, what should you do? Your first goal should be understanding the sources of your emotions and behavior. Insight into your sibling dynamics—the causes of your conflicts with brothers and sisters—will be the key to making sense of your uncle/aunt–nephew/niece relationship. The issues present may well revolve around your view of yourself as a Good-Enough Sibling, your role as a Supersibling, or your experience with your niece or nephew as an Invisible Sibling. Consider each of these possibilities to see which one may be pertinent. Grasping the dynamics will help you have a relationship with your niece or nephew that's less entangled with sibling issues.

Being an aunt or uncle can be an opportunity to celebrate what is treasured in the sibling relationship as long as you can filter out your own negative sibling issues. This opportunity holds especially true when the nephew or niece seems to "echo" a brother or sister with whom you already have a strong bond. Aunts and uncles can share in the intimacy of parent-child bonds without all their work and fatigue.

A close relationship with a nephew or niece can be a positive force for everyone concerned. As Yvonne found with Taylor, such a relationship can give the niece or nephew additional adult attention, love, and support; it can provide the uncle or aunt with the special delights of a child's company; and it can serve as a further tie between brothers and sisters.

Holidays—and "Hellidays"

The regularity of holidays offers a potential advantage: at least you know they're coming. Even so, their cyclical arrivals and departures can create cross fire and fallout in their own right. This isn't to say that holidays aren't great fun. Obviously they are times of deep satisfaction, playfulness, and joy for many families. Yet most families find that at least some holidays have a dark side, too—a side that affects sibling relationships as well as other family ties. This dark side may even overshadow the sweetness and light of festive occasions and make the holidays real "hellidays."

Sometimes a holiday proves stressful simply because it throws people together who might otherwise avoid one another. Caroline found that holidays gave certain of her relatives who ordinarily didn't talk the opportunity to corner one another and air whatever grievances had accumulated over the years. "There was a lot of verbal abuse," she recalls of such occasions. "Lots of undercutting. And they would do what I call the 'and furthermore.' If you had done something that had displeased them, it was trotted out. 'And *furthermore*, your complexion is terrible!' 'And *furthermore*, you don't have any boyfriends!' And *furthermore* . . .' "

At other times, the conflict is more specific, perhaps even carrying over from one holiday to another. Blake, Adele, and Gerry are adult siblings. Adele has felt protracted resentment toward Gerry, her younger brother, for a long time. Ten years ago, when the siblings were planning to attend their parents' Thanksgiving celebration, the smouldering conflict exploded. Gerry had promised to drive Adele to their parents' place, but he never showed up. Adele missed the dinner. For all the years since, Adele has been furious with Gerry. Blake has attempted to mediate the conflict but without success. In fact, he has gotten caught in the cross fire. Gerry and Blake recently hosted a retirement party for their father, but Adele boycotted the festivities. She was sniping at Gerry because of the long-resented Thanksgiving fiasco, but her father and older brother caught the "bullets."

One of the main reasons holidays are difficult is precisely that our expectations for them run so high. Many people tend to see holidays as times of affirming family values and ties. But what family can consistently live up to the pressure that everything will go well, that everyone will have a splendid time? Eat, drink, and be merry! Revel in the joys of parenthood, childhood, siblinghood! While you're at it, celebrate the unsung virtues of unclehood, aunthood, niecehood, nephewhood, and cousinhood! 'Tis the season to be jolly—and sometimes the pressure to be jolly makes it anything but fun.

For grown siblings, these high expectations have unusually heavy consequences. There is often a sense of tension between your long-gone but easily remembered childhood role and your current role as an adult with your own career, social circle, home, and perhaps family. Sometimes the past and the present clash. For some people this can be hard precisely because they feel tension between who they were and who they are. It's not at all unusual for adults to find that holidays create discomfort as they revisit the family home in the company of brothers, sisters, and other relatives.

Consider Samantha's experience. She is the marketing director for the New York office of a large international bank. She's professionally ambitious and accomplished. She lives alone but has an active social life. Thirty people report to her at work, and she frequently visits her bosses and colleagues in Europe. Yet when she goes home for family holidays in the small southern city where she grew up, Samantha often feels inadequate, misunderstood, and harshly judged.

"Thanksgiving and Christmas are excruciating" she says. "My family treats me as if I'm returning after a summer at camp. 'Are you eating enough?' 'Have you found a boyfriend yet?' 'When do you think you'll move back to a safer city?' My parents and my sisters talk to me as if they know what's going on in my life. But they don't. They know nothing about my life, my work, my friends, or my life-style. They have no idea what New York is like or why I want to live there. Yet they assume I'm who I was a long time back—Samantha the southern belle. And I don't tell them what I *really* am because they wouldn't understand."

For Samantha, these interactions are always a strain. She was the Black Sheep of her family long ago; now, having fought long and hard to redefine herself, she finds that holidays challenge her not to lose her sense of who she is; she wants to avoid getting slotted into the Black Sheep role again.

This situation is typical of the clash of roles that sometimes occurs during holidays. When you go home for visits, you may face expectations that you'll click back into your old role; or—worse yet—expectations *that you never changed in the first place.* These expectations are problematic whether you meet them or not. If you meet them, you may please your parents and siblings but resent the situation. If you refuse to meet them, you may cause resentment by resisting family "authority." As Caroline puts it, "Holidays always louse people up—that's what they're for."

Another factor that makes holidays into hellidays is the old sibling rivalry issue of who comes first. Precisely because holidays focus on

140

the importance of family, they heighten expectations of receiving love and attention. If you feel that you aren't receiving your fair share, it can create hard feelings. The same holds true if you feel that your children aren't getting their fair share of attention from family members compared with what your sibling's kids are receiving. There's a constant concern over who feels more important and who's in charge. In short, holidays may set off or intensify power struggles between individuals or groups in a family, which often derive from sibling rivalry, with people feeling slighted, or emotionally shortchanged.

In addition to feeling that you're not getting the close attention you want, you may simply feel you've been replaced. Seeing your siblings in family settings may highlight how much your relationships with them have changed.

Terri's family had a long-standing tradition: on Christmas Day, everyone used to visit one relative after another. During adulthood, she and her husband and children would combine forces with her brothers' and sisters' families to meet at Terri's childhood home; they would then form a caravan of cars to make the rounds. But last year Terri's sister refused to take part. She decided to stay put with her husband's family in a nearby town. "I'll swing by on Christmas Eve," she said, "but I'm not going to buck the traffic on Christmas Day." Terri felt furious and hurt. She had to work Christmas Eve; she wouldn't be around if her sister came only that night. More to the point, however, she felt hurt by her sister's plan. "Her husband's family seems to matter more than her own," Terri says, "and I won't get to see her or my little nephews."

Although you gain a lot when you have nieces, nephews, and in-laws, the feeling of being replaced can occur. Many sisters and brothers end up feeling overlooked, undervalued, or hurt during the course of family festivities.

Finally, there's a complicating factor that arises out of personal and family history. Holidays are by definition cyclical events. "Christmas comes but once a year"—but it does, after all, come year after year. The same holds true for holidays in other traditions. For this reason, and because they are times of emotional intensity, holidays tend to be highly evocative. Whenever you celebrate a particular holiday, you're both dealing with the intensity of the here and now and being aware of the memories of holidays long ago. This is especially true for the most emotionally loaded holidays in each tradition: Christmas and Easter for Christians; Passover, the High Holy Days, and Hanukkah for Jews; Ramadan for Muslims; and so forth. People often remember the wonderful times they've had during some distant holiday, but they can also remember the occasions when family members fought or when no one had a good time. Among these recollections are memories of sibling conflict, expressions of rivalry, and so forth. These memories color what's happening in the present. Old emotions and incidents emerge unbidden. If your brother does something mildly insensitive this Thanksgiving, it may upset you; but you may feel far more upset because of what his behavior evokes from your interactions thirty years earlier.

What emerges from all these aspects of the holidays is that among the good times now you may feel fallout from past sibling conflicts. Then the caustic ash of past fires may ignite new conflicts. Anger, resentment, and hostility flare up, apparently out of nowhere. Yet in fact the holidays have made a mixture of high expectations, sibling rivalry, and past grievances so combustible that any little gesture or action can spark an explosion.

None of this should come as a big surprise. Holidays are great fun, but many people find at least some holidays problematic, even traumatic. There's even a psychological term for the blues that many people experience after major holidays: postholiday letdown. Given the complex reality, though, what can you do to deal with holiday difficulties and how they affect you and your siblings?

Short of moving your family to a deserted tropical island and establishing a culture in which birthdays, national festivities, and religious observances are all prohibited, here's what I suggest.

First, put the holidays in perspective. Remember that they are special occasions, and they have their own norms for behavior. Despite the complex windup for some of them, they come and go rather quickly. Enjoy them for what they offer; brace yourself for what they demand; then move on. Most important, take what happens with a grain of salt. It's a given that many traditional cultures regard holidays as occurring in a kind of time different from what regulates ordinary events. Anthropologists even speak of rites and celebrations running on "sacred time"—a flow of events that differs markedly from normal time. People in such cultures often consider life itself as departing from its usual constraints on such occasions. The normal rhythms of the day (adults' work, children's play, and family activities) are suspended. An example is the celebration of Mardi Gras in parts of Europe, most of Brazil, and America's own New Orleans. This wild festival is a time when ordinary life comes "unhinged" and people behave for several days in a freer, more emotional, often wild manner.

Even within the more restrained customs of mainstream American culture, holidays do something similar. This is important to note because, in our secular era, we've made our celebrations more like our regular lives—hectic, expensive, and competitive—than they used to be. As a result, we often expect our family members to behave as usual; we expect them to mean just what they would have meant under normal circumstances. If you can remember that holidays are out of the ordinary—that is, that they are extraordinary days—you may feel more tolerant of what goes on at such times.

Remember, too, that you're going to have to "stretch" emotionally to maintain your role as an adult. You will be challenged by many people's assumptions and expectations about you, any one of which could open old wounds of sibling rivalry. You'll have to work on staying focused on your adult role to avoid falling back into your childhood family role.

Despite your tolerant attitude and mental focus, however, conflicts may still arise. For instance, I can't tell you how many of my patients have said to me, "How am I going to deal with my sister?" or "How am I going to cope with my brothers when I see them?" or "I'm still so angry I can't face her."

Here are some strategies that you can implement to emerge unscathed.

My best advice is *be prepared*. Do not go naively to a holiday celebration. Instead, consider the nature of your relationships and the feelings you have toward your sisters and brothers. Try to reflect on who might say or do something to antagonize or upset you. If you're anticipating an attack, try to head off your brother or sister to the greatest degree possible. A big family bash is one of the worst possible times and places for a heart-to-heart over old resentments or new misunderstandings. You won't have much (if any) privacy. The setting will only make matters worse. The solution: stall for time.

As early as possible, take your sibling aside and say, "I really want to talk with you about what happened. It's on my mind, too, so we should get together." That is, frame your comments to acknowledge your sibling's desire to talk, but don't capitulate to the insistence that you hash it out then and there. Emphasize the need for an appropriate time and place: "We should do this in private and with enough time, okay? Let's make a date to get together next week." By handling things this way, you've given a message of affection and concern. You're not shutting out your sibling with a rebuff: "How *dare* you bring this up now?" Yet you've made it clear that now isn't the time. "We need more time—this is too important to crowd in now. And it's too important for us to spill with everyone else watching."

A sibling may also attack you out of the blue. "You're such an idiot!" your brother shouts. Or your sister asks, "How could you have said that last week?" Or your brother screams, "You're so selfish!" If you suffer a sneak attack, how do you deal with your sibling's unexpected anger and your own anger—not to mention the public embarrassment?

This is probably the most difficult situation to handle. You're caught with your guard down. Not only has your brother attacked you but he's attacked at a time when you're supposed to be having fun. Worse yet, he's attacked with all sorts of people watching and listening. At such times it's hard not to feel both angry and startled.

Siblings sometimes broach awkward topics by coming in sideways, attacking you with an understated insult, a sharp-edged joke, or some other comment that makes their anger evident but doesn't allow you to respond without seeming oversensitive. This is the "slap shot" attack.

It's not overt—yet you've been assaulted. "What happened to your hair?" Your sister asks. Or your brother comments, "Looks like you gave up on that Exercycle, didn't you?" Such remarks stab you with one statement while hinting at (but not presenting) a hidden agenda.

Counterattack is an understandable temptation. Unfortunately, though, it's the worst possible response. As before, the setting couldn't be less auspicious; any insult or angry response to a sneak attack only adds fuel to the fire. In the case of slap shots, your retorts do nothing to get at your sibling's hidden agenda.

So what's the answer? Obviously, it's dousing the flames. This is a lot to ask of yourself or anyone, but it's not impossible. This is an ideal time to respond rather than react to what your sister or brother is telling you. Comment on your sibling's behavior rather than react to your emotions about that behavior. If your sibling has made a nasty remark, comment on his or her observational skill instead of flaring up over what has been observed. In short, focus on what your sibling is doing to you rather than on the content of what he or she is saying. For instance, if a sibling says, "You've put on a lot of weight" or "You're so self-absorbed," your response should be something like "Well, you never miss a thing" or "It doesn't surprise me that you noticed" or "It's good you pointed that out—I might have missed it." Focus on your sibling's need to observe rather than on what he or she has observed.

Does this strategy solve the problem? Not in the long run. However, it spares you the task of dealing with criticism and anger in the midst of a hopelessly complex social setting. Work your way toward a suggestion of discussing things later.

Sibling rivalry conflicts between adult brothers and sisters can create cross fire and fallout that can harm not only you and your sibling but your spouse, children, other relatives, and friends as well. When you're able to resolve some of your conflicts, however, or at least to understand their origins more clearly, the multiplicity of ways that you and your siblings influence one another can prove more satisfying.

Part Three

Other Significant Dimensions of Siblinghood

————————

10

When a Sibling Marries—
New Strands (and Strains) in the Sibling Bond

Imagine for a moment that you're talking with a friend. She's describing a wedding she recently attended, and she mentions how much the groom looks like the bride's father. What's more, the bride has the same first name as the groom's mother.

Would this story surprise you? Probably not. It's not exactly a secret that our parental relationships influence our choice of marital partners. Many people marry someone who resembles their parent of the opposite sex.

Would it have surprised you if your friend commented that the groom looks just like the bride's *brother*? Or that the bride has the same first name as the groom's *sister*? Maybe not. But maybe so. Somehow we're not quite as likely to assume that our sibling relationships have equal influence over our marital decisions.

If you're skeptical, consider Joy. Joy married a man who has the same last name as hers. Coincidental? Perhaps. But her husband also has the same first name as Joy's brother. And he bears a close physical resemblance to her brother.

Often people date or marry partners who have the same name as their sister or brother. For example, Kent's first wife was named Linda—as is his sister. Now Kent is divorced and planning to remarry;

his wife-to-be is also named Linda. Sometimes people choose partners whose names are similar to or derivatives of a sibling's such as a man with a sister named Joanne who is dating someone named Joan or Jean.

Or consider Eve and Brett. Not only is Eve the same age as Brett's sister Julie but, the two women have the same birthday.

Or Evan. "My sister Elaine and I have always been close," Evan explains. "She's my closet friend, and has been ever since childhood. You might say she's my image of the feminie ideal." Evan admits outright that this closeness with Elaine influenced his decision to marry Megan—who resembles his sister both physically and emotionally.

The list could go on and on. People often date and marry people who strikingly resemble their siblings in age, appearance, name, and manner. In fact, the similarities are often so obvious that they are totally overlooked. After you have spent your whole childhood with your siblings—people from whom you learned about fair play, identity, cooperation, communication, and family roles—it's not at all surprising that they strongly influence your choice of a spouse. After all, your spouse becomes your adult companion and playmate. Furthermore, the number of brothers and sisters you have may influence the number of children you and your spouse decide to have, as well as the timing of when you have them. It may even influence your choice of names for them. It's not unusual, in fact, for people to choose to have a family configured much like their own family of origin, or for them on occasion to name their children after siblings.

Sibling relationships affect marriage, just as marriage, affects sibling relationships. The influences are more numerous and more powerful than most people recognize—ranging from the initial events of getting married through events during marriage and even to the consequences of getting divorced.

Getting Married

Regardless of their genuine delights, weddings aren't always events of undiluted joy. In fact, getting married often creates upheaval for both members of a couple and their families. Assumptions that weddings shouldn't be tumultuous or problematic can make them all the more so.

We often think of getting married as volitional: whom we marry is a matter of choice. Although choice certainly plays a large role, other influences—some unconscious—enter into our decisions as well. What makes sibling influences on marital choice so significant is that they are more common and powerful than we imagine, and we generally are unaware of their consequences.

Additionally, your siblings' expectations of your marriage partner may create tension in your family. If your brothers and sisters don't approve of the spouse you've chosen, you may feel torn. You may place more of a premium on your siblings' opinions than you'll readily admit. The situation is all the more difficult if your parents disapprove as well.

For instance, Ida intended to marry Kenneth, a biologist she had met in college. Kenneth's background, interests, and personal manner differed greatly from what Ida had grown up around. Whereas Kenneth was a loner fascinated by science and the arts, Ida's parents and brothers were extroverts who loved sports, parties, and big family get-togethers. Kenneth's visits with Ida's family never quite worked out. Her parents and siblings were outwardly hospitable but clearly uneasy with their potential in-law. Ida got the message early on that her parents and her brothers all disapproved of her choice of a marriage partner. No one did anything direct—in fact, everyone made an outward show of warmth to Kenneth—but Ida detected her family's opinion all the same. Ultimately, the situation created enough strain that Ida's loyalties to her parents and brothers won out over her commitment to Kenneth.

Why is marriage so often full of obstacles for sisters and brothers? When your brother or sister marries, you experience an abrupt and often substantial change in the nature of your relationship. You may even experience the loss of companionship. Your brother's availability will be more limited and less spontaneous than it was. When your sibling marries, you may lose the sort of interaction you had before. You will almost certainly lose the *degree* of interaction. If your brother has married, his primary relationship will be with his wife. He'll be spending most of his time with her, and rightly so. But where does that leave *you*? Or perhaps your sister marries. You remain emotionally close, but the days are over when you can just call her up and talk without time limits or spontaneously suggest, "How about if I come over right now?" Your support system has changed, and these changes can't help but affect you. For example, Arlene's brother Drew got married several months ago. Only now is she feeling the full effects of this change in her life. She can't just stop by any evening to visit with her brother, as she used to for years, since Drew now wants to spend time mostly with his wife.

Another aspect of marriage is one or more siblings remaining at home when a brother or sister marries and moves out. Depending on the circumstances, the marriage changes the sibling bond. Tensions can run high; negative feelings can intensify. When Gwen was getting married and leaving home, for instance, she got in an argument with her sister, Cassandra, that eventually escalated into a full-scale war. Gwen yelled, "You're just jealous of me because I'm the one who's getting married, and I don't want you coming to my wedding!"

In addition to jealousy and rivalry, siblings may feel an array of other emotions. Some of the most compelling are those of being displaced and replaced. A sibling's marriage can create a sense of being nudged—even shoved—out of one's rightful place in relation to that brother or sister. At times these are even feelings of being abandoned or deserted, including a sense of losing uniqueness and importance in relation to your sibling—and perhaps to your family as a whole.

There may also be a loss of role. Suppose your younger sibling has just gotten married. You may feel you've lost your role as protector, as controller, as the one who knows best. This loss may prompt you to feel that you've lost your own identity, self-esteem, and importance.

Since he was five and his sister was born, for example, Brad had always looked after Josephine. He loved her, delighted in her, protected her. He wanted everything good for her and thought more about her happiness than about his own. Then, at the age of twenty-two, Josephine married a man ten years her senior. Brad felt so abandoned and disappointed in his sister's choice of a husband that he stopped talking to her for years.

The flip side of this situation may hold true as well. Suppose your older brother or sister has gotten married. You may feel the loss of a protector, role model, or guide. The nature of the loss will depend on your sibling relationship and specific roles; however, the experience of loss and the changes resulting from it can be dramatic and powerful.

If you're getting married, or if your brother or sister is getting married, how should you deal with the problems that may develop? How should you cope with the intense emotions, old rivalries, and outrageous behaviors that can flare up precisely when you're expecting supportiveness and family bliss?

A good starting point is to keep in mind the difference between the wedding and the marriage. In almost every respect, the marriage is what matters; the wedding is just the rite of passage. But when the festivities themselves are taking place, it's not hard to imagine that the wedding makes all the difference and the marriage is a mere afterthought. This isn't to say that the wedding is insignificant. Rather, the point is that it's easy for family members—including sisters and brothers—to lose a sense of proportion. Even the most extravagant wedding will last only a few days. The ensuing marriage may last for decades. Weddings evoke a lot of strong feelings, and these feelings matter, but sibling warfare triggered by the wedding may jeopardize potentially close relationships in the long run.

What intensifies the situation is that siblings are often major players in a wedding. A sister may be maid of honor; a brother may be best man; sisters and brothers may be involved in every phase of preparation and in the ceremony itself. Siblings are drawn into the celebration and affected by the event and its long-term influences on the family. It's understandable that siblings can be both major allies and major troublemakers at a wedding.

How do sisters and brothers respond to these occasions? It's important to emphasize that in most families people rise to the occasion, play their parts, enjoy themselves, and do whatever they can to help the bride and groom have a splendid time. If a few feathers get ruffled, everyone takes it in stride. However, even in happy families the nuptial road can be more than a little bumpy, and siblings are implicated in some of the bumps.

As already noted, the problems often originate in old sibling conflicts, rivalries, or assumptions about roles. But whereas marriage allows a continuity of time during which siblings can sort out their differences, the wedding is a brief event with everyone's emotions at fever pitch. The potential for misunderstandings and outbursts is great. The opportunity for sorting things out on the spot is limited. Small wonder that weddings may seem like crises. They sometimes *are* crises!

Jessica's wedding is a case in point. At the reception, Jessica and her husband were to have the first dance; then the rest of the bridal party, including Jessica's brother Marshall was to join them. Yet Marshall couldn't be found anywhere; everyone just stood around waiting for him. Jessica sent a friend to look for him. Marshall turned out to be socializing elsewhere in the catering hall. Needless to say, Jessica felt hurt and angered.

Marla, who had spent many years in conflict with her sister, Mia, did everything possible to make Mia part of her wedding. In fact, Marla hoped the occasion might bring the two sisters together. Yet when Marla was dressing for the ceremony, Mia acted oblivious. She never complimented Marla on her gown or any other aspect of the preparations. Mia kept asking how *she* looked without acknowledging Marla in any way. Four years later, Marla still hasn't gotten over her sister's behavior.

In short, all kinds of sibling issues crop up at weddings. They aren't the end of the world, but even so, they're badly timed and frustrating, the last thing you need when you're about to undergo one of the great traditional rites of passage.

So if you're getting married—or if your brother or sister is—how should you deal with the sibling issues that surface at the time of the wedding? Your response depends a lot on the specific circumstances, of course, but several steps can make life much easier. (Note, too, that the same issues that can make your wedding tumultuous for your siblings may make a sibling's wedding tumultuous for you.)

Perhaps the most basic step is to recognize that weddings mark a time of tremendous change. No matter how exciting, such occasions are unnerving, unsettling, even frightening. Out with the old and in with the new! Weddings are stressful for more than just the bride and the groom. It's not hard to imagine that your parents will be shaken by the changes that a wedding signals, but keep in mind that you and your siblings will be affected too.

In addition, keep in mind that your marriage may hold far more intense personal meanings for your siblings than you first thought. The same will hold true for you when they get married. Your wedding may jolt your brothers and sisters into insights about where they are in their own lives, about their relationships with you or other family members, about their feelings of sibling rivalry, envy, and resentment. To the degree possible, be sensitive to what your sisters and brothers are experiencing as your marriage changes your relationships with them, or as their marriages change their relationships with you.

It's also helpful to put events at the time of the wedding into a wider perspective. Perhaps you and your siblings are lashing out and treating each other inappropriately because of being unable to deal with intense feelings about the upcoming wedding. Understanding the situation won't take the hurt away, but it will help contain anger so that it doesn't contaminate the wedding.

Do your best to take these difficult incidents not as insults but as opportunities to deal openly with the situation. This is a tall order when you have your mind on other matters, and when many people around you have their own agendas. But if it's at all feasible, talk over the situation—sort through the issues—early on so that you can prevent misunderstandings that may otherwise simmer for many years.

Remember: the wedding may be a major event, but it's just the start of the marriage itself. The wedding is supposed to be a beginning, but for many siblings it feels like the end. Even sibling relationships that seemed irrevocably damaged by a brother's or sister's marriage may change for the better.

During Marriage

After the wedding comes the task of coping with the impact that marriage has on both you and your siblings. The heart of the matter is understanding the dynamics that make marriage hard not only for the couple but for other family members as well.

Many of the conflicts that arise between brothers and sisters after their weddings are extensions of sibling rivalry and the issue of "fair share"—often expressed more directly in the lament "You've got more than I do!" How each sibling continues to measure up goes in tandem with how the marriage "rates."

Another point of contention may be the timing of the marriage. In some families there are assumptions—even rigid expectations—about who gets married first. Generally the expectation is that the older children will marry before the younger. Even if the siblings claim to have disengaged from such traditions, their emotional responses may prove otherwise. If a younger sibling marries first, the older ones may feel resentful. The same may hold true for the timing of having children, as well as for the number of children each sibling has. This competition can also extend to questions of whose mate is more attractive, whose mate has more money, and whose mate's professional or personal attributes seem to put him or her "ahead" of the others. These are all forms of outdoing or feeling outdone by one's sibling.

For example, Wanda talked about her sister as if life were one huge episode of "The Price is Right." "She always has more. Her marriage is the perfect marriage. Her husband is more handsome than mine, and richer, and more sophisticated. They have the perfect house, the perfect car, the perfect jobs, the perfect children. She always *wins*."

Our sisters and brothers also have a big impact on the quality of our marriage relationships, whether for better or worse. Feelings between siblings often carry over into the brothers' and sisters' marriages. Many people don't realize, for instance, how often they inadvertently re-create with their spouse strong aspects of their sibling relationships. Heather and Marty came to me for marital therapy. Among their complaints was Marty's resentment of how Heather talked to him. She constantly put him down; he felt offended by her tone. In the course of treatment it emerged that this was exactly how Heather behaved toward one of her brothers. She didn't mean to insult her husband: abrasive talk was simply how siblings communicated in her family. But the carryover from brother to husband created a serious conflict. Or consider Sandy, who sums up certain aspects of her marriage in these words: "I often thought I was mothering my husband, but now I realize I was sistering him."

Another significant way in which siblings influence marriages is in the effects of birth order. Aside from the obvious fact that our brothers and sisters are part of our family solar systems, whose gravitational fields still tug at us, the research of Walter Toman on family constellations illuminates the importance of sibling relationships in marriage.

Toman devised the Duplication Theorem, which postulates that the more closely someone's marriage resembles earlier relationships—particularly those with siblings—the more likely it is to be happy and successful.

An important aspect of this theorem is what Toman calls complementary relationships, in which partners complement each other in terms of birth order and gender. For example, Betty is an older sister to Jonathan, who is younger by four years. Betty's husband, Allen, is a younger brother with a sister three years older. Because Betty and Allen "match" in the same pattern as each does her or his sibling, their relationship is complementary. Toman also speaks of partial complementarity. By this he means that the match approximates a sibling pairing. For instance, Kathy has a brother five years older than she is. She married Ned, who is five years older and has a younger sister. However, Ned also has an older brother. While this relationship is not an exact match (since Ned has an older brother as well as a younger sister), it is close enough for Toman to call it partial complementarity.

Toman's theorem suggests that marriage partners with greater complementarity will get along better than those with less. Why? Because each spouse will to some degree relate to the other in a way that's familiar from earlier in life. Imagine a wife, for instance, whose sibling role as the oldest sister was to be highly motivated, organized, energetic, and forthright. She likes taking the initiative and setting most of the agenda. By contrast, her husband, as a youngest brother, tends to be easygoing, relaxed, and comfortable following someone else's lead. Or perhaps the husband is the leader; the wife is the follower. Either way, their family backgrounds and consequent attitudes may strongly influence how they deal with the world, including each other. And their complementarity may increase their ability to share their life and all its activities.

Consider the inverse of this situation: partners who are alike. An example would be George and Alice, each of whom is an oldest sibling. Both have the common firstborn characteristics of ambition, intensity, and goal orientation. They go about life in much the same way but tend to compete and bicker. Within their marriage, each wants to be the leader. Their marriage may be close and good, but it may generate sparks. What's the implication? That the more closely partners resemble each other—such as these two firstborns—the easier it may be for them to empathize with each other; at the same time, however, it may be more difficult for them to coexist.

Regardless of family size, the configurations for complementarity are constant. It's secondary whether you're the middle child of three or one of the nine "middle" children of eleven. The same holds true for youngest children, whether one or a dozen siblings showed up before.

Toman's research data confirmed his notion of sibling-role combinations. Of 2,300 families with children, 5 percent were divorced, which corresponds with the overall population's divorce rate, while among those with complementary sibling roles, there were no divorces.

Here's another variation on the theme. Kevin Leman, author of *The Birth Order Book*, often gives seminars on how birth order affects our relationships. At these seminars, he divides everyone in the room according to their birth order. Oldest, middle, and youngest children cluster into separate groups. Leman then provides each group with paper and pen to make a list of their common traits. What is the outcome of this exercise? In more than two hundred seminars, these groups have behaved in predictable ways. In the group with the youngest siblings, no one picks up the paper. They're all waiting for someone else to get organized and make the list! The middle-born children take a little longer; then someone takes the initiative and the group gets down to work. But among the oldest, someone always picks up the list right away. In fact, members of this group are often competitive over who takes the lead.

Dealing with Siblings-in-laws

In addition to the stresses that can exist between siblings, in-laws complicate matters further. We call them in-laws, but for many people they seem like outlaws. In-laws can usher in strong feelings of jealousy and resentment that spring from the issue of exculsivity.

Issues of exclusivity and importance come into play in all marriages. We all have a need to feel important to our mates. We hear this need when a wife complains, "My husband is always working—he's not home enough" or "He's always watching sports." Or we hear the husband complain, "She's always out with her friends" or "She pays more attention to the kids than to me." Each of us wants attention and appreciation. Feeling appreciated gives us a sense of well-being. Such feelings are basic to a marriage; they are essential to its long-term health.

One way people cope with a sibling's marriage and the new reality of sharing their brother or sister is by trying to reclaim their old relationship. Perhaps you dislike your sibling's mate; perhaps you feel that his wife or her husband is somehow "not good enough" for your sibling; perhaps you resent the loss of companionship brought about by his or her marriage. If these are your feelings, you should consider two important aspects of the situation.

First, jealousy is a two-way street. Although you may envy the time your sibling now spends with his or her spouse, you may be the object of a similar envy. The spouse may even view you as a rival for your sibling's affection. Especially during the early years of a marriage, the need to "share" someone with the wider family may be stressful. Be aware that others too may be experiencing confusion at a time of change.

Second, heavy demands of your married sibling tend to create an either-or situation. It's as if you're demanding, "Choose him or me!" Yet this is a terrible bind. Few husbands or wives will tolerate this sort of ultimatum; nor should they. The sibling relationship is so different from marriage that pressuring for a choice (even when the pressure is unintended or unconscious) places excessive strains on everyone. In fact, the situation should be not *either-or* but *and*. Your brother needs to be able to have his relationships with his wife and with you. Your sister needs to be able to have her relationships with her husband and with you. Carefully considered, the situation should allow room for each person to feel important and appreciated in the context of his or her particular relationship. You need to hold on to your priority of reshaping your sibling relationship rather than make impossible demands that back the relationship into a corner.

The in-law relationship can often become an extension of the sibling relationship, with all its inherent pluses and minuses. In-laws can readily heighten the intensity of sibling rivalry and become a forum for old conflicts, so that disagreements and misunderstandings get battled out through the in-laws rather than between the siblings themselves.

Consider the case of Leigh and Bill. They've been married five years. In many ways they're close and happy. Bill's brother Tony, however, is a major point of contention between the partners. Tony is three years younger than Bill and highly competitive with him. The brothers are frequently at odds, but they are also closely involved in each other's lives.

The most recent issue is that Tony is getting married. In preparation for the wedding, Bill suggested to Leigh that they pay for the rehearsal dinner. "Tony can't afford it," Bill told Leigh. "Besides, it would be a nice gift for us to give him." Leigh was furious. Why should they spend money on Tony when they were financially pinched already? Also, they'd never done anything like this for Bill's older brother, nor for any of Leigh's siblings. And Tony hadn't given them a gift for their engagement *or* their wedding. Leigh and Bill have argued over this decision for weeks.

Worse yet, they've argued for years over Tony and his role in their life. Why must they travel so often to see Tony in Phoenix? Why does Tony have an open invitation to visit when Leigh's siblings don't? Leigh resents the inequality of the situation. She resents Bill's excessive availability to his brother. Most of all, she resents Tony himself. Tony's latest antic is that he's marrying a woman who has the same name as Leigh and is entering the same profession. The race is on. While Bill and Tony are working on their sibling rivalry, Leigh is wrestling with the issue of exclusivity and feeling angry because she doesn't seem to come first in her husband's eyes.

Leigh feels that Tony is too intrusive in her life with Bill; he consumes too much time, attention, and money. In this kind of situation a spouse winds up feeling that a brother or sister is more important to his or her partner. This belief can trigger tremendous jealousy, rivalry, hostility, and resentment that lead to arguing, measuring, and comparing in numerous ways. Another difficult situation arises when the Supersibling role prevails: If a sibling constantly needs help getting out of trouble or in some other way requires support and assistance, the sibling's needs can wreak havoc on a marriage.

Another form of sibling rivalry battle occurs when the in-law becomes the "hit man." This is when the in-law steps in and fights the siblings' battle for them without either the siblings or the in-laws realizing the nature of the conflict or why it's occuring. For example, one of my patients, Ricki, is married to a man who refuses to let Ricki see her sister. Ricki is rightly infuriated by this prohibition. Her husband, Steve, certainly has no right to ban his wife from visiting her sister. But the situation is more complex than it seems. In fact, Ricki has felt angry at and frustrated with her sister for years, but she has avoided communicating this anger directly. Instead, she attempts to deal with her emotions on her own. Steve ends up fighting Ricki's battles for her.

There can be many variations on this theme. For example, Margo and her brother Mike are very close, but Margo's husband, Barry, can't stand his brother-in-law. He refuses to socialize with him; as a result, holidays and other family occasions are troublesome. This situation creates a strain in Margo's marriage. When this occurs, the siblings themselves may get along, but the in-laws wind up at odds with each other. This tension often is an expression of unresolved or unaddressed sibling rivalry. Because siblings place such a premium on getting along, they may be out of touch with some of their negative feelings toward each other. In situations of this sort, the in-laws can become unwitting fighters of a proxy war.

If these conflicts focused on a friend, the marriage partners might be able to resolve the problem by agreeing to cut off contact with the offending party. But with siblings it's different. You can't disown your relatives—at least not without tremendous upheaval. Husbands and wives often want to outlaw their in-laws but can't. What results is a double toll: first, there's strife between the marital partners; second, there can be erosion of the sibling bond.

Eleanor felt that she wasn't getting enough companionship and attention from her husband, Dave. She and Dave fought bitterly for a long time over his prolonged phone conversations with his brother about business dealings. Eleanor was furious that her brother-in-law was getting the attention she wanted. Finally, she confronted her husband. Dave then agreed to spend each evening with Eleanor and to call his brother only when he wasn't with his wife.

In essence, in-laws can become sparring partners for sisters and brothers who continue to compete over who is best, who has the most, and who really comes first. But coming first may mean taking turns, not being the sole focus of attention. That is, legitimate rights to your sibling's or spouse's attentions are not equivalent to *only* rights. Positive relationships acknowledge a multiplicity of interpersonal contacts.

If you have a feud with one of your spouse's siblings, try to determine what might be missing in the relationship with your spouse that you could remedy. Eleanor figured out what she felt was missing in her marriage, then talked things over with her husband. Dave eventually was able to set limits with his brother that greatly strengthened his marriage.

If in-laws strife hampers you—that is, if you are caught between your spouse's and sibling's needs—setting limits with your sibling can be useful. In order to do so you must remember that you can be a Good-Enough Sibling even when you place limits on your availability to your sister or brother. You can't always carry the responsibility to make things fair; instead, you must figure out what you need to do to avoid being pulled into an untenable position.

If you are a sibling with a married sister or brother, you can begin to deal with being an in-law by recognizing the loss that you've experienced. One way to deal with this loss is to find new ways to become involved with your sibling. Heather is a good example of this option. In the early years of her older brother Howard's marriage, Heather realized that she wouldn't see him as often as before. She resented her sister-in-law for limiting the time that Heather now had with her brother. She spoke with Howard, however, and soon he began treating Heather as a peer rather than as his little sister. For the first time in five years, he invited her to the couple's beach house to share a vacation. This allowed Heather a new but satisfying form of involvement with her sister-in-law.

As with other points of contention, in-laws require clever balancing. Acknowledge that both you and your spouse's sibling, or you and your sibling's spouse, have legitimate needs for time and attention. Try to negotiate the limits of these needs in ways that serve all parties. Accept the need to balance your conflicting priorities. To the degree possible, set limits in ways that constrain unreasonable expectations and ease the resultant tensions. For example, if your spouse needs time with his brother but you find getting together with him too emotionally demanding, work out a compromise. You might say, "By all means see your brother. Take some time with him. I'll join you for the first hour, then you can visit by yourselves." You can use the rest of the time for some personal activity, such as gardening, shopping, or whatever else interests you.

When a balance can be achieved, relationships with in-laws can be wonderfully rewarding, even healing, by offering an opportunity for a fresh start if you've had a poor sibling relationship. In effect, they can become positive Invisible Siblings. After extended sibling conflicts, for instance, James found that he had hard feelings not just toward his brothers but toward men more generally. He found his friendships with other males strained, sometimes hostile, and consistently limited in both number and depth.

James married in his midthirties, and his marriage has been overwhelmingly happy. Morever, as he grew comfortable with his brothers-in-law—two near his age, one about ten years older—he found these relationships salutary in many ways. In addition to being satisfying in their own right, his almost brotherly closeness with his brothers-in-laws has allowed James to reexperience congenial feelings such as fraternal competition. James has even discovered that friendship with these three men has put him more at ease with male-to-male friendships in general.

Here's another instance. Tammy found that her marriage created not just one close bond but a network of family ties. "I'd known my husband since the seventh grade, though we'd dated other people," she says. "It was my brother who kept saying, 'He's really a good guy.' Then my brother married my roommate, who was someone I'd suggested he should meet. I kind of lined him up because I thought they'd be wonderful together. We're all very compatible. We even send our kids back and forth. It's still very harmonious."

These examples suggest the possiblities for growth and, as Tammy notes, harmony in in-law relationships.

Dealing with Divorce

Divorce can profoundly affect the brothers and sisters of those whose marriages have foundered. The effects of a sibling's divorce can be either positive or negative—often unpredictably so. Some people may rise to the occasion, thus renewing or strengthening a sibling bond. Others may find that their sibling bonds deteriorate or even break under the stresses common during divorce proceedings; this seems especially likely if one member of the divorcing couple looks to siblings for support and feels disappointed by a meager or nonexistent response. Old sibling rivalry issues are likely to resurface. Concerns about who comes first and who's getting a fair share will be expressed by a sibling who expects both financial and emotional support. Your sister or brother may even want you to take a stand against her or his spouse.

Sometimes a divorce can cause siblings to fall back into the old roles of Big Brother, Big Sister, Protector, and so forth. For example, Lee relied on her sister Rhonda as her Protector till she got married. During Lee's divorce, Rhonda once again assumed that role. In her effort to be supportive, Rhonda became so protective that she intruded on Lee's intense personal situation. Rhonda even reprimanded Lee for getting divorced. Rhonda offered support but in a form more appropriate to her old role—making decisions for her younger sibling—rather than providing what her sister needed as an adult: reinforcement for her own decision. As a result, Lee and Rhonda felt such hostility toward each other that their bond was strained just when Lee needed it most.

Divorce also affects in-law relationships. Sometimes it is possible for in-laws to maintain their relationships, which may have become friendships with a life of their own. For instance, John went through a bitter divorce from his wife, Pat. But John had always been close to Pat's sister Georgia. John and Georgia were able to stay friends, a positive experience for both of them. In other instances, however, the allegiances can be served if a sibling remains in contact with an in-law. One of my patients, Debbie, told me that, as she and her husband divorced, it was vital to her sense of well-being that her brother (who had become friendly with her husband) "choose her" to the exclusion of her now ex-husband. In this case, Debbie's brother agreed; their sibling relationship took precedence.

Archie and Meg met in high school and married soon after. During the early years of their marriage, they often baby-sat for Meg's younger sister Susan, and Archie developed a close friendship with his sister-in-law. But Archie and Meg divorced twenty years later—a change that threatened to end Archie's tie to Susan, now in her early twenties. Archie despaired over the loss of both his wife and his sister-in-law. The situation was difficult until he found a way to preserve his bond with Susan. Archie explained to her, "Our relationship is really important to me. I'd like to find some way of continuing it." In fact, he wanted to remain involved in her life without Susan feeling that she had to choose between him and Meg. Susan was receptive; she reciprocated Archie's feeling that the relationship was important. She'd work it out with Meg, she said. Susan added that she was glad he had talked with her because she had worried that Archie would cut off their relationship as a consequence of his divorce.

Finally, divorce can create issues concerning nieces and nephews. Even if someone feels no strong emotions about his or her sibling's divorce, there may be deep regret, anger, and loss over an end of contact with the nieces and nephews.

Divorce, stressful as it may be, doesn't simply cut the bonds between husband and wife. It also severs ties between other relatives—among them siblings of the spouses—who may have a high stake in the relationship. If you can stay aware of the various issues of sibling rivalry that may flare up at this time, it will be easier to cope with the resulting expectations and demands. Divorce can even become an opportunity for strengthening or renewing your sibling bond.

11

When a Parent Dies

One of the most intense crises that siblings face is a parent's death. The intensity isn't just a side effect of grief and bereavement; it's also the result of how a parent's death changes the nature of siblings' relationships to one another. After a parent dies, brothers and sisters rarely see one another in quite the same way.

Before delving into the specific nature of these changes, however, we should consider more generally what happens during the course of these complex family events.

The Crisis of Illness and Death

A mother's or father's illness and death are among the times that test the bond of siblinghood. If the bond is vulnerable or fragile before the parent becomes ill, the stress of this crisis can damage or even break the relationship. But this crisis can also strengthen or reshape the sibling relationship. Even a sibling bond that has its share of difficulties can end up stronger following such a crisis. In short, the tasks of dealing with a sick parent can have either healthful or harmful effects. Sometimes siblings rise to the occasion; sometimes they don't. If they offer one another relief, reassurance, support, comfort, and a sense of solidarity, they may renew or deepen their mutual respect.

For instance, Veronica found that her family's crisis pulled everyone closer. "Mom had lung cancer that spread to her brain, gradually leaving her unable to care for herself," says Veronica, who spent a lot of time with her mother during her seven-month illness. So did her dad, one of her brothers, and her sister. "Sharing Mom's illness with my family was a very meaningful experience. My sister and I were always close. I feel sorry for my younger brother because he had Mom the shortest time. But I respect and love him even more after seeing how he used to travel frequently—eight hours back and forth from graduate school—for even just a one-day visit. We are closer now than ever."

If, though, brothers and sisters are unable or unwilling to help one another, the bond between them may deteriorate, and a cold war may erupt. When their mother died, Jay offered little help to his sisters, Agnes and Helen. They felt so furious about Jay's distance that they refused to communicate with him for several years.

The main reason a parent's illness and death so powerfully influence how brothers and sisters feel toward one another is that during this sort of crisis the longing for siblinghood grows more intense than ever. First, caring for a parent may exceed what any one person can accomplish. Siblings need to cooperate. Second, such a family crisis may activate old feelings about what siblinghood ought to be, and siblings need each other at such times. Third, illness and death may intensify the issue of which sibling is responsible for specific tasks. The result is a shock to siblings both individually and together. Brothers and sisters often truly need one another when the going gets tough; at the same time, they have a heightened expectation that sisters and brothers should pull together. The combination of needs and expectations intensifies most people's sense of what should happen at a time of crisis.

Louise felt great distress as her mother grew more and more debilitated during a severe illness. Louise knew that it was only a matter of time before she would have to move her mother into a nursing home; there was no way she could care for her alone. She knew as well that her brother and sister would essentially wash their hands of the situation. After all, Louise was (as they reminded her) Mother's favorite.

Yet Louise felt overwhelmed by the practical and emotional repercussions of the task before her. She needed her siblings' help to provide the attention their mother needed. Despite her efforts to engage their help, however, both her sister and her brother remained aloof. Ultimately their attitudes irrevocably altered Louise's relationships with her siblings.

In this situation as in many others, keeping the balance among siblings requires constant attention. This is often difficult precisely because old roles, family favoritism, and sibling rivalry start to influence siblings' sense of who is responsible for what.

For example, Faye's mother was chronically ill. Faye was going to share the responsibility of taking care of her with an older brother. However, the brother said, "I can't have her come and live here. I have my children and my wife to consider—I just can't do it." He reneged on his end of the deal. About three months later, their mother died. Faye hasn't talked to her brother for three years; she's too angry at him for having shirked his responsibility.

These reactions are all by-products of the crisis itself. When a family member falls ill or suffers an accident, almost everyone will enter a state of intensified emotions. Fear, helplessness, and anxiety are all common and normal components of this state. If nothing else, most people feel overwhelmed by the inordinate number of decisions that need to be made: medical, financial, legal, and interpersonal decisions are often jumbled together or taken in quick succession. Sometimes siblings even have to make critical decisions about whether to continue, change, or suspend a parent's medical treatment—choices with literally life-or-death consequences. Who is the best doctor? Which hospital should Mom be in? Who should handle the money matters? Should Dad go into a nursing home, or should one of the family take care of him at home? Under circumstances such as these, it's no wonder that siblings feel a lot of stress.

As in so many other situations, part of what makes these sibling interactions successful or unsuccessful has to do with roles. The crisis of a parent's illness can bolster siblings' relationships *if* they pull together and divide the responsibility in accordance with each one's personal or professional strengths. This is not unlikely if everyone can be flexible about roles. Perhaps you were the Kid Sister during childhood, and everyone treated you like a know-nothing. But now you're a successful businessperson. Will your siblings move past their old assumptions about you and trust your advice on how to handle Dad's finances? Or perhaps you were once the family Black Sheep but are now an accomplished physician. Will your brothers and sisters listen to your suggestions regarding Mom's medical treatment? At times, no matter how you may have changed during adulthood, your siblings will continue to see you in your old role. You may be a physician, but your brother and sister insist on seeing you as a pretender. If they are able to see you in a new light, however, and if you in turn move beyond your old perceptions of your siblings—you may all be able to stretch into more constructive, creative roles. In so doing, you will not only deal more successfully with the crisis, but also have a chance to renew and reshape your sibling bonds.

But the reverse is true as well. If you and your siblings cling to old perceptions and act out old roles, then your ability to cope with the crisis may be more limited. You may also damage your sibling relationships still further. Perhaps as the Kid Sister you hesitate to offer your opinions and expertise: you fear that the others won't accept what you contribute. Perhaps as the Black Sheep you can't get your medical insights across. Perhaps you begin to feel "out of the loop"; the decisions are still being made without you. Or perhaps you aren't able or willing to let your sisters and brothers move beyond *their* old roles into something new.

In such situations, where old roles dictate what people will or won't do, everyone's freedom to act ends up limited. Big Brother wants to visit Dad but feels that his past rebellious behavior has made him unwelcome. Middle Sister would like to relinquish her role as the Supersibling and help in a more balanced way, but she worries that her siblings won't offer enough help to take up the slack. Little Brother wants to contribute money for their parents' medical care but wonders if his siblings will resent his financial success; however helpful his contribution may be, what it represents in terms of the "fair share" may rub the others the wrong way. In these situations, financial security can be a double-edged sword. Siblings may resent you if you contribute more money simply because of your ability to do so; yet they may resent you as well if you refuse to foot the bill when you have the resources to do so. Not only can these "tight" roles limit behavior, but they can also lead to rips and even ruptures of the sibling bond.

Our culture tends to regard crisis solely in negative terms. Other traditions, however, give the word a different meaning. The Chinese character that represents "crisis," for instance, also means "opportunity." In other words, a crisis may bring trouble, but it also provides the possibility of change. The family crisis triggered by a parent's illness and death can often present a valuable opportunity for positively altering sibling relationships. Acknowledging this opportunity does not belittle the genuine tragedy that gives rise to it. A parent's death is a great loss; nonetheless, many people find it an impetus to change in themselves as well as in their close personal relationships. Facing loss can create a desire to replenish what is gone with new meaning. When siblings deal with a parent's loss, they often have a chance to repair or build new relationships with each other.

If a sibling relationship is going to be vital and continuing, it must keep changing. The sibling relationship that never changes will stagnate, and the brothers and sisters in that relationship will become stuck in it rather than freed by it. But how can you deal with the possibility for growth when you already have your hands full?

One of my patients, Ben, had been estranged from his older brother, Tom, for many years. Ben and Tom stayed out of touch by choice, and they didn't get along when thrown together during holidays and other family occasions. Each had a satisfactory relationship with their parents, but neither could shake the old roles that constrained their sibling relationship and defined their mutual resentment. Ben was the strong, authoritative Firstborn. Tom was the indecisive, irresponsible Rebel. So it had been; so it would always be.

Then their father had a major heart attack. He made it through the initial crisis, but his long-term survival was in doubt. The brothers flew back to their hometown to assist their mother and visit their father. At first the old frictions caused lots of trouble: each brother got on the other's nerves, resented the other's presence, and questioned how much help the other was contributing. Then something happened.

"These were life-and-death decisions we were making," Ben told me in therapy. "I'd always been the older brother, I'd always taken care of Tom, I knew what to do. But now, in the middle of this mess, I didn't feel I could handle what was happening alone—either emotionally or concretely—nor could I really grasp the long-range ramifications. Dad might well be dying. How should we handle this situation? Which hospital should we put him in? Which doctor should do the surgery? I didn't know. It wasn't that I was incompetent—just that I couldn't do it all myself. Meanwhile, Mother was saying, 'I don't want to move him; let's just leave him here.' But Tom and I saw that this wouldn't work. The hospital wasn't so great. We didn't trust the doctor. Looking back on it now, I'm sure Dad would have died if he'd stayed there. So we had to do *something*."

Ben continues: "Tom is a doctor. I'd never really faced up to that before. My kid brother is a doctor! And I know more about financial stuff than he does, so I had my own two cents' worth to contribute. Somehow we saw what had been there all along—we're both adults now, capable and competent—and we were better off joining forces than fighting. So that's what we did. And together we were able to wade through all the choices and options and help Mom reach some decisions that none of us would have made alone. We moved Dad to another hospital and got him the right kind of care. It saved his life. He's fine now. But if we hadn't worked together, we would have been overwhelmed. The truth is, I couldn't have pulled this off myself."

Ben and Tom actually accomplished even more than saving their father's life. They also saved their fraternal bond. Or rather—and better yet—they transformed it from one based on rivalry, resentment, and mutual belittlement to one based on cooperation and respect.

Dealing with a Parent's Illness and Death

When an interpersonal crisis occurs, the resolution will have one of three outcomes.

One possible outcome is a change for the better. Members of the relationship may develop new strengths and abilities for dealing with each other. The relationship may resume at a deeper level. In terms of siblings, a balance may evolve that leaves each more in tune with the other. As Sharon told me after she and her sister joined forces to help a sick parent, "I was never close to my sister. We were always far apart on everything. But I really saw her in a new light, and I got involved with her in a new way." Among the reasons people give for such improvement are that siblings felt their bond was more intense or more appreciated; they seemed more supportive or involved than before and shared decision making; they spent more time together, moved to be geographically closer, or expressed more emotional closeness; they learned to communicate better, shared their feelings, expressed pain, sadness, or compassion, and stayed in touch more frequently; they found that previously damaged relationships began healing; and they sensed their own or each other's roles changing—for instance, an older sibling became more respectful, while a younger sibling became more cooperative.

The second possible outcome is a change for the worse. The family members' strengths and abilities for coping may be so tenuous that the crisis is debilitating. The people involved may end up with a damaged relationship. With siblings, this means less interaction, less respect, less interest. Dina put it like this: "I always thought that my middle sister was a responsible person, but she was so uninvolved when our dad was ill that I just can't respect her anymore." The reasons people often give for negative changes are that siblings resented each other; they felt burdened by family obligations; they drifted further apart; they felt blamed for their lack of involvement with a parent, criticized for the quality of their involvement, or blamed for causing the parent emotional distress; they felt angry about either the practicalities of the other siblings' involvement or the unavailability of the other siblings; and they felt an upsurge of sibling rivalry.

The third possible outcome is no change at all. There's no improvement; there's no decline; everyone just muddles through. The crisis may resolve itself, or people may enter a time of crisis but not deal with it, and the crisis may simply pass. An older sister summed up her situation in this manner: "Right after our mom's accident, we all pitched in. But within a few months, when things settled down, all the pieces fell right back to where they were." For better or worse, the situation remained as before.

The factor that creates the second and third outcomes is role stasis. Role stasis is what you experience when your present sibling relationships are based on the roles you acquired as a child or adolescent—roles which you have outgrown yet which (at least in your siblings' eyes) you haven't shed. That is, the roles are motionless, changeless, lifeless—though you yourself have continued moving, changing, and growing. You may be a perfectly competent adult in your usual settings; however, when dealing with your siblings, the fact that they see you in your old role may precipitate your falling back into old attitudes and behaviors. You become irritable, annoying, or inept when interacting with your sisters and brothers. The diversity and flexibility you've developed collapse into rigidity or impatience. In short, the old roles have placed you in a kind of behavioral atrophy. You feel trapped by expectations that are a thing of the past.

If these descriptions suggest either how you feel around your siblings or how they seem to feel toward you, the consequences in a family crisis may end up messy and frustrating. You may, for instance, find it difficult to take a proper share of responsibility. Or you may take too much responsibility but resent your sisters and brothers for taking less. Or you may act properly under the circumstances but find that your siblings criticize you despite your good intentions. "You don't know what you're doing," they say, or, "Why aren't you pulling your own weight like the rest of us?" Role stasis can leave you feeling either excluded or overburdened.

An especially clear sign of role stasis is when one sibling feels stuck with all the responsibility or all the work. If you're the sibling who's feeling burdened in these ways, you should try to determine how you see your role in relation to your siblings. Consider these questions: Are you doing your fair share of the work in caring for your parent? More than your share? Less? Are your tasks determined by your abilities and responsibilities, or by assumptions based on past roles? Are your siblings delegating work to you without forthright discussion of what seems best for all of you and for your parents? Are they delegating work simply by refusing to take responsibility for their own fair share? Are you doing what you do out of genuine desire, or out of a sense of obligation and guilt?

Facing these questions and attempting to answer them honestly may be ways of getting a better handle on the crisis facing all of you. Admittedly, the task isn't easy. But it's easier than dealing with protracted misunderstandings and subsequent cold wars based on roles that have been obsolete for years—even decades. Not only that: facing these issues can also help you understand or redefine your sibling relationships. This, too, is a difficult task. But, again, remember that a crisis offers the potential for positive change.

A parent's death is part of the normal sequence of life events, but many people seem to equate its being natural with its being inconsequential. In fact, many people find a parent's death difficult for both emotional and practical reasons. And these difficulties include its effects on sibling relationships.

One of the most common tasks facing siblings after a parent's death is dealing with the will. If the second parent is still alive, this task may be less intense; however, probate in all its intricacies may still be one of the brothers' and sisters' responsibilities.

One popular image of siblings in the aftermath of a parent's death goes something like this: the dour-faced brothers and sisters sit in a lawyer's office; the family attorney reads the will; each member of the family listens closely, alert to the slightest inequity in his or her share of the spoils. Fortunately, the situation isn't often so bleak. Many families settle the issues of probate in a businesslike, amicable way. Yet the situation definitely has its pitfalls, and it's a genuine source of tension and misunderstanding in many families.

Sometimes fighting is predictable because it's an extension of the sibling relationship. Wills and the shares of material wealth they bestow are perceived as equivalent to personal value, worth, love, control, and power. Many people assume that if you have more of something (possessions, love, parental attention), then I have less; if I have less, then I am worth less; if I am worth less, then I am worthless. Many people see money as a sign of love and will see a sibling inheriting more money as meaning that the sibling was more fully loved than they were. While in some cases a larger bequest may indeed indicate favoritism, in others it may mean that one sibling is simply less able to provide for himself or herself than the others. Rather than revealing favoritism, it's an extension of the parent's role of providing for a child. However, even an actual indication of parental favoritism is an expression of the parent-child relationship, not of the relationship between siblings.

Psychologically speaking, this means that the true issue isn't the money or other bequests—real estate, furniture, personal possessions, and so forth. Rather, the issue is what these things symbolize. Your deceased parent's worldly goods seem like stamps of approval (or disapproval) on you as a son or daughter. But do the funds or items we inherit truly say what we imagine they do about who we are? About what we are worth?

Consider these dimensions of the situation: Your inheritance says something about the relationship between you and your parent. It does not refer to your sibling relationship. What happens after your parent dies is an extension of what happened during your parent's life—between you and your parent. This isn't to say that your parent-child relationship doesn't affect your sibling relationships. If one child has been favored and another scapegoated, and if these biases have been perpetuated in the will, then there clearly will be consequences for the sibling relationship. But it's important to keep in mind that it's not your sibling who caused the misunderstandings

178

or difficulties. You may have legitimate gripes against your parent. But you won't help yourself by taking them out on your sisters or brothers.

In addition, these situations can provide a chance to understand your family better, and thus to heal old wounds. Sometimes a difficult family situation changes when a parent dies. As much as you may grieve over your parent's death, the new situation may allow you opportunities to repair or forge your sibling bonds. Sometimes, for instance, parents' expectations force brothers and sisters into uncomfortable roles. When a parent dies, you may be able to define your relationships according to what you and your siblings want, not just what your parent wanted.

Here's an example of a sibling conflict over an inheritance which was really a conflict between each of two children with their father. Dominic had two sons, Leo and Nick. When Dominic died, he left all his money to Nick. His rationale was that Leo had become involved some years ago in a business venture that Dominic disapproved of because Leo had invested too much money in it. Dominic believed (rightly) that Leo would sink all his funds—including any inheritance—into this investment. He didn't want his money going to finance a long shot. After Dominic's death, Leo felt furious not just at his father but at his brother as well. Nick in turn feels angry at Leo for his resentment, since the will and its consequences weren't his fault; he's also hurt and angry that his father put him in such an awkward position.

The only chance for resolution between these brothers is if they can realize that what has happened is not a statement about their relationship as brothers; rather, it's a statement about the relationship each of them had with their father. Neither Nick nor Leo should blame the other for what has happened; they should recognize instead the nature of their individual father-son relationships, then go forward with their lives.

Parents express many emotional undercurrents when writing their wills: love, anger, vindictiveness, favoritism, guilt, desires for power and attention, and any number of other evident and hidden agendas.

What parents do with their wills is often a complex, messy matter. And it's not just a legal matter, but a psychological one as well.

The aftermath of a parent's death takes many people by surprise. We may assume that becoming adults has put us beyond the range of grief when a mother or father dies. However, this simply isn't true. No matter what our age, this event hits hard. Loss is a powerful experience, and even the most self-sufficient man or woman may be affected by it. As the Scottish psychologist E. E. Wilkie once stated, "The loss of parents is one of the great watersheds in life."

Many of the emotional issues siblings face with each other when their parent dies have to do with the differences in how people experience bereavement—that is, how they feel following the death of someone they love. Others stem from how they express their grief. Still others concern the changes that come about as a result of bereavement.

Bereavement is the reaction to the loss of a close relationship. This process is part of being human; in some respects it's the cost of our capacity for emotional commitment. The most conspicuous aspect of bereavement is grief, which is the emotional expression of loss (sadness, longing, bewilderment, and so on). The consequences for someone dealing with a loved one's death are important but often ignored.

Grief is normal. Although painful, it is generally a sign of emotional health. Moreover, grief is a process, not a brief and tidy event. Coming to terms with a loss takes time. Grief does not come and go overnight—or even in a few weeks or months. Some major losses (the death of a spouse, lover, parent, sibling, child, or close friend) may have emotional repercussions for years. Finally, grief is varied. People experience loss in various ways. There is no one way, no "right" way to grieve. Some people express their emotions openly; others are self-contained. Cultural traditions affect how people grieve, but so does individual personality.

What these aspects of grief mean when brothers and sisters deal with a parent's death is that each sibling will experience the loss differently, and each will express his or her emotions differently. For some, expression may be withdrawing from family activities, in some cases including refusing to attend the funeral. Different manifestations of grief are as normal, predictable, and healthy as different manifestations of joy; however, many families find the variety of grief a source of difficulty at a time of crisis.

Discord between siblings following a parent's death is regrettably common. "My brother was not available for the moral strength and decision making required of me. I resent him for this—he almost completely deserted me at the time of Mother's short illness and death. He went fishing the afternoon of her funeral and the next day while I closed up her apartment and sorted out her belongings. I am sure this was the only way he could handle things. But I am still angry."

Lack of cooperation during the crisis is probably the most common sore point. Perhaps certain brothers or sisters provided care and others didn't. Matt felt that "lack of assistance from my only brother created a rather hard feeling." Cynthia experienced conflicts with both her sisters: "I got mad at my sister who lives out of town for leaving all of it to me. The other sister worked full-time, so I got all the problems."

Brothers and sisters who get along during a parent's illness and after the death aren't unusual, but neither are siblings who end up bickering or resenting each other. High expectations of sibling harmony probably complicate the situation. Ironically, however, you and your siblings may be the last people capable of helping each other. This isn't in spite of the shared loss but because of it. You and your siblings are suffering the same stresses. You are physically and emotionally depleted in the same ways. Why should you be the perfect allies during your struggle? What each of you wants and needs—an optimistic outlook, patience, clear perspective, and abundant energy—is precisely what all of you lack.

In addition, your parent's illness and death may well evoke long-forgotten (or perhaps well-remembered) issues of sibling rivalry. Powerful old feelings combine with the more immediate tensions. The result is a strain on relationships. It's not surprising that brothers and sisters have difficulties getting along when parents die.

First, here are some specific suggestions for dealing with siblings when a parent is ill or dying.

It's particularly important to *stay aware of the wider issues in your family*. What are the old expectations about how family members should act, who should do what, what is proper behavior at times of crisis, and so forth? What are the assumptions about roles? Do these assumptions free you and your siblings to act in mutually helpful ways—or are you constrained by how all of you see one another? What old conflicts may be complicating your current situation? Being aware of these issues doesn't solve all your problems. But if you are alert to them and conscious of their potential effects, you can at least know that you're on a roller coaster. This knowledge gives you a chance for a safer ride.

As the crisis takes shape, *take stock of where you are with your siblings*. Are you estranged from your sister? Do you still see your brother in his childhood role, or as the adult he is now? Are you and your other sister on good speaking terms? In short, take an inventory of the overall situation. This overview gives you a sense of where you stand with each member of your family; if nothing else, it gives you some perspective. It also helps you tell which problems are old and which are the result of this crisis.

In addition, *try to discuss all issues openly to the degree possible*. If you haven't spoken to your sister in years, if you haven't gotten along with your brother, if you've been fighting with him for months, then you're better off acknowledging your differences from the start. Discuss the situation as early as possible. Again, such discussions may not be fruitful, but, by knowing where you stand, you at least have a chance to address the family issues rather than just watch them unfold. You can identify obstacles and steer around them. You can tell your siblings, "Look, I know there's a rift between us. We've been fighting for years. But can't we just put this aside for now, with the understanding that we'll deal with it once we're through the crisis? Let's get through this mess together. Let's agree to disagree, let's help out Mom [or Dad], then let's get back to our own disagreements."

In addition, several approaches can make grief more manageable in the aftermath of a parent's death. (This holds true no matter whose death you are grieving.)

Remember that grief heightens emotions. You and your siblings are under stress, and your reactions even to everyday events may be more intense than usual. Problems that seem insoluble now may look easier to deal with in a few months.

Keep in mind that grief is highly individual. Some people withdraw, some people become remote, some people get angry, some people get very practical. Each of you has a right to your own way of grieving provided you don't impose on the others.

Try to keep issues separate. A conflict over an apparently practical issue (such as selling the family house) may have deep emotional roots. If you can determine where one issue ends and another starts, you'll have a better chance of dealing with them successfully.

Consider seeking an outsider's viewpoint. You and your siblings may have such strong emotions about the aftermath of your parent's death that you aren't seeing events clearly. A trusted aunt, uncle, other relative, family friend, pastor, or counselor may be able to provide insights that all of you lack at the moment.

Take care in speaking your mind. Bereavement can provide an opportunity for speaking with rare candor—an opportunity often well worth taking. But candor has its risks. Ultimatums, dares, and threats during a time of emotional intensity may drastically compound the damage your family has already suffered.

Remember the side effects of physical and emotional fatigue. Even a brief family emergency will strain both your body and your mind. A protracted crisis can exhaust you. How can you get through the long haul? As simplistic as it sounds, you have to take good care of yourself. Get as much rest as you can; eat well; pace yourself. Also, keep in mind that physical and emotional fatigue will affect your perceptions and decision making. This holds true for your siblings as well. You may all end up so depleted that you're unaware that you're not seeing straight. Wait for things to settle down before expressing your emotions.

Admittedly, these suggestions reflect ideals to strive for, not goals that all families can attain. Sometimes roles are too rigid. Sometimes expectations are too specific. Sometimes conflicts are too deep, too old, too durable to overcome on short notice. All you can do is try. Your siblings may or may not respond to your efforts to simplify the task before you. You can't *make* them understand the advantages of an open mind. But you can offer your insights and hope for the best.

12

Growing Up Twins

Twins experience what other siblings do but far more intensely, for twins share everything—even their birthday—in a setting of acute family scrutiny and heightened expectations. Simply by virtue of being twins, they feel the glare of a spotlight focused on them from the start. The sibling relationship and its delights and difficulties are therefore greatly intensified for twins.

Even if you aren't a twin, the issues affecting twins may be relevant to you. There are, for instance, many situations that create what I call pseudotwins—siblings whose relationships have dynamics similar to those existing between twins. One sometimes occurs when parents remarry, since newly blended families may include stepsiblings of similar ages or even the same age. Another takes place when parents adopt a baby and soon after conceive their own child. Yet another occurs in cultures that encourage families to raise children who are very close in age as if they were twins. Finally, circumstances such as some siblings' close physical resemblance may prompt parents to treat them more like twins. In any of these situations, parents may find that their children's relationship evolves into something like twinship and that other members of the family experience side effects similar to those occurring in a family with twins. Although what real twins experience is much more intense, the issues that affect them may affect pseudotwins as well.

Twins and Rivalry

Twins' inherent similarities and constant companionship often turn up the heat on rivalrous emotions. Intense sharing is an integral aspect of being a twin. Twins first share their mother's womb—a remarkable experience in its own right. Then, as babies, they share their parents' time, attention, and nurturance. As toddlers, they may share toys, clothes, food, and other material and nonmaterial family resources. As Mindy, an identical twin, put it, "We were like one. We shared everything together, including our baths." During the school years, twins may share their teachers', peers', and parents' attention. They are immediate contemporaries at every stage; they reach developmental milestones more or less simultaneously, thus heightening competition for whatever material or emotional resources are in demand.

Parents' feelings about having twins dramatically influence how twins regard their twinship: whether they value or devalue it; emphasize or minimize it; enjoy, resent, or even ignore it. The world loves twins and often tends to give them disproportionate attention. Accordingly, many parents also feel great delight in having twins. Those who do may play up twinship. They may dress their twins alike, give them similar names, heighten their twins' similarities in any way possible. These parents experience tremendous pleasure and gratification in how the world responds to them for having received a double blessing. Alternatively, some parents resent having to deal with two children at once. Some mothers of twins have expressed feeling a loss of the bonding experience with one child at a time. These negative feelings can cause parents to minimize the significance of twinship. Each parental style (that is whether emphasizing or minimizing twinship) may affect twins and how they feel about themselves.

Another issue that affects twins' relationships is comparison. Non-twin siblings confront this issue; however, the experience is far more constant and extreme for twins.

From birth, all twins are compared with each other. When people learn that children are twins, they characteristically focus—sometimes with great intensity—on the twins' similarities and differences. The situations differ for identical twins and fraternal twins. (Identical twins develop from a single ovum; fraternal twins develop from two ova). With identical twins, people focus more on what makes them similar. Are their features the same? Do they speak alike? Do they share temperament, habits, and tastes? This constant comparison can increase identical twins' developmental closeness because it intensifies their sense of common ground. With fraternal twins, however, people tend to look more for the differences. Fraternal twins must endure remarks like "You don't look like twins at all—he's so much taller." This constant focus on differences can inadvertently fuel competition because one twin always seems to come away better off.

The focus on either similarity or difference can intensify twins' own sense of how much they are like or unlike. That is, repeatedly comparing or contrasting twins can put a premium on similarity or difference, so that the twins actually strive even harder to be similar to or different from each other.

All identical twins resemble each other to a remarkable degree; some fraternal twins resemble each other as well. To be so similar to someone else creates pressures that nontwins can scarcely imagine. On the one hand, similarity allows a degree of safety; on the other hand, it threatens to diminish the individuality children crave as they grow and develop. The result is often a tremendous internal pressure. And the pressures differ for identical and fraternal twins, with important consequences for their bond.

Other siblings put up with comparisons of their attributes, among them physical appearance. Whom you look like in the family often influences with whom you become identified. As a result, your identity derives partly from your appearance, including your similarity to one or more members of your family. This similarity may become a means for closeness with (or distance from) siblings or other relatives. The situation for twins is even more powerful. For the many sets of twins I've spoken with, the most distressing and wearisome experience of twinship is being compared with each other.

Whichever twin was born first gains special status and power in the family—even if the first birth preceded the second by no more than a few minutes. This notion sometimes sounds ridiculous to anyone in a family without twins. How can it possibly matter which twin is older when you practically have to mark the difference with a stopwatch? In fact, it matters enormously. First is first. Period.

"I'm ten minutes older than my twin brother," says David somewhat boastfully. "That was always a big joke in my family: I'm the older brother! But on some level we took it seriously. Dylan and I were very close—went everywhere together, did everything together—but I was still the first among equals."

This sentiment is not at all unusual among twins. If anything, the issue of birth order is more significant with twins, not less so, precisely because there are so few other differences between them. Birth order plays into the desire for individuality. This is true for fraternal twins but all the more important for identical twins, for whom birth order becomes a prime distinguishing feature. It's not the two minutes that matter; it's what those two minutes represent symbolically for the older child. The older brother or sister often inherits certain family expectations, allegiances, advantages, and roles. Even a few minutes' seniority brings the same advantages and pressures (and sometimes far more of each) that a year's or even ten years' age difference brings to nontwins.

At times this issue is so powerful that twins can deal with it only by denying its existence. Jeremy and Jonathan are twins who claim not to know which of them is the older. "The hospital lost the records," Jonathan explains. "Jeremy might have come first. Or maybe I did. We're not sure. Actually, it makes no difference—it's really not an issue for us."

Even when parents have just one child, one of the first questions they hear from relatives is "Who will you name the baby after?" Implicit in this question is "Whose side of the family?" The naming of twins can be even more highly charged than it is for other children because it draws invisible lines of alliance to respective sides of the family; in addition, it can prompt the twins themselves to feel a stronger attachment to one side or the other. One twin may inherit a name from the father's clan, for instance, while the other inherits a name from the mother's. The result can be sibling rivalry focusing on who has more attention from one parent or the other—or even on who "belongs" to one or the other. Since parents often see twins as a "set," it's not uncommon for them to feel (though perhaps not consciously) that "that is your twin; this is my twin." Regardless of whether parents are aware of these alliances, the attachments they generate may be strong and deep.

Names—particularly those for identical twins—may also generate strong attachments between the twins themselves. For instance, many parents give their twins matched or rhyming names—Jim and Jerome, Thomas and Tim, Lucinda and Lucille, Cindy and Mindy, and so forth. These names may strengthen the twins' bond.

The Twin Bond

What makes being twins so special is in fact precisely this bond: the unique emotional tie that twins forge by sharing each other's companionship literally from the moment of conception.

For identical twins, one aspect of this bond is biological: they have the same genetic nature. Studies on identical twins raised separately done at the Minnesota Center for Twin and Adoption Research show patterns of remarkable similarity in interests, likes and dislikes, mannerisms, and life events. In some cases, both identical and fraternal twins are so close that they manifest what can only be described as paranormal communication—an ability to sense each other's thoughts, emotions, and actions even without direct contact.

What's most significant, however, is that the twin bond is a byproduct of how twins deal with the fundamental issue confronting all brothers and sisters: sibling rivalry. Twins deal with both the positive and the negative feelings inherent in siblinghood in several ways. These ways often correspond with characteristic twin roles.

When they are already dealing with the stresses of twinship, the heightened attention to physical similarities can pressure twins into declaring a truce of equality. As formulated by several theorists— among them D. T. Burlingham, E. J. Hirt, and D. W. Orr—this truce is usually an unstated understanding that things will be kept equal between the twins. They may ultimately avoid situations in which one stands out at the other's expense. If they compete, it is in areas where both excel, so that the chances of one beating the other are minimal. In its strongest sense, twins will do things that celebrate what I call twindividuality—the special sense of identity shared as twins—over individuality. Such a truce of equality is a way to constrain rivalrous, angry, resentful feelings about what one twin has that the other doesn't. With this truce comes a stress on similarities over differences. A truce of equality deepens the investment in twinship. The result is a more consistent perception of twinship as a blessing.

The roles that often emerge from the truce of equality are what I call The Twins. The Twins are those whose identity is almost totally wrapped up in twinship. These are the twins who often or always dress the same, wear the same hairstyle, go everywhere together, and in every other respect find most of their energy and sense of purpose in being twins. Their twindividuality is more important than their individuality and at times may eclipse it.

For instance, Karen and Sharon are identical twins. They look exactly alike, dress alike on occasion, and do almost everything together. They share friends, clothing, homework, household tasks, and all their playtime activities. It's hard for them to imagine doing anything apart. Although their parents are supportive of their closeness, school officials have often found it unnerving, even to the point of trying to keep the girls in separate classes. However, these efforts have been so disruptive for everyone—most of all for Karen and Sharon, who languished academically as well as emotionally when kept apart—that they are now back in the same classroom.

At times the role of twins puts severe strains on twins' individual perceptions. Meryl and Sheryl, nineteen years old, are identical twins who have always stressed their similarities. Both are beautiful, but Meryl at some point became dissatisfied with the shape of her nose and pleaded with her parents to let her have plastic surgery. Unfortunately, the results of her operation weren't what she'd hoped for. Meryl had a second nose job, then a third. As a result, her face became somewhat disfigured. Meryl was understandably distraught. But Sheryl was too. The twins were no longer identical. It was a tremendous loss for both of them—as if *both* had been disfigured. And, in terms of their twindividuality, this is precisely what had happened. Their relationship had been disfigured because their twin bond of equality and the sense of identity they derive from it had been disrupted. Now each twin had to derive more of a sense of who she was from her own individuality.

Another kind of twin bond is complementarity—that is, when twins divide areas of experience in ways that complement each other. Several theorists—including D. T. Burlingham, D. B. Jarrett, Maureen McGarty, and D. H. Ortmeyer—have acknowledged this bond. In the bond of complementarity, each twin defines certain areas as his or her own—tastes in food, toys, clothes, or playmates; interests in school, sports, or other activities; social skills—with an understanding that they won't enter each other's areas. In addition, they agree that this allotment will be to their mutual advantage.

It's almost as if they've developed a system for being in two places at once. In effect, the twins have nonverbally agreed on occupied zones. For example, you develop a greater degree of interpersonal finesse and feel more comfortable making friends. Your twin, meanwhile, shows a more solitary, private bent. You take up sports; your twin excels in school. Under the best of circumstances, this allows you to "cover more territory" than either of you could separately. Each of you accomplishes something for both of you. By this means, complementarity becomes a way of sharing experience rather than competing for it.

Complementarity has both advantages and disadvantages. By spreading both the responsibilities and payoffs, twins limit the stress of their twin bond. Complementarity contains the rivalry, hostility, guilt, and aggression that all siblings feel. Ideally, twins divide up areas of experience in ways that are mutually agreeable and satisfying.

The areas may or may not overlap. There's a sense that "this is yours, this is mine, and we both possess it."

William and Wyatt are identical twins who were emotionally close during boyhood but different in many ways. William is sociable and outgoing. Wyatt is more reclusive and academically inclined. Their disparate interests have allowed them a diversity that they might not have attained separately. William handles all the twins' social plans; he meets people easily, sets up dates, breaks the ice. Wyatt, meanwhile, keeps track of the twins' academic situation: he tutors his brother in math and science, writes reports for both of them, and generally manages the twins' intellectual life. By handling separate aspects of life, William and Wyatt feel that they are able to be in two places at once.

However, one twin may feel limited by the allotment of areas. Complementarity can develop less by conscious design than by gradual accretion. The arrangement creeps into place during childhood, most often as nonverbal assumptions. No documents are signed—the terms aren't even discussed. They simply *evolve*. As a result of these occupied zones, each twin misses out on a realm of human experience that could actually belong to both. You may value a sense of unity rather than your separate interests, abilities, opinions, feelings, and needs; or, as you grow older, areas or territories that you consider "yours" can begin to change, either by your design or by your twin's. If your twin suddenly begins to express interest in one of your realms of activity, you may feel that your territory has been invaded, with a consequent increase in rivalry and mutual resentment.

For example, Sadie and Kadie came to me for therapy. Both were entertainers who had learned to dance as children. During adolescence, the sisters divided up the territory of their artistic pursuits. Sadie was the actress, who starred in every class play; Kadie was the dancer, who charmed everyone at her recitals. This division worked well until Sadie and Kadie reached adulthood. Sadie went into modeling and became quite successful. Kadie continued dancing and joined a prominent modern dance troupe.

Both thrived in their careers. However, after several years, the twins' occupied zones shifted, and trouble ensued. Kadie found that her body was suffering the strains of dancing. She decided that she would shift into modeling too. Without discussing this transition with Sadie, she began to audition for magazine shoots for which only one twin could be chosen. Sadie found out and was outraged. This was her zone! How dare Kadie show up for an audition! The twins had tremendous battles. What helped them come to terms with their rivalry and anger was understanding the unspoken nature of their territories, as well as recognizing how their boundaries were changing. Sadie and Kadie needed to talk about this situation. Their subsequent discussions made it possible for them to get past their anger and make room for both of them.

I call the roles common among twins who have forged a bond of complementarity Tweedledum and Tweedledee. These are the twins who put some emphasis on their twinship but also stress some differences. They may share interests and activities, but they go their own way too, with considerable pride in their independence.

Another common outcome for twins' sibling bond is what I call indifference. This occurs when twins refuse to acknowledge that twinship is an issue for them at all. "Oh, we don't pay much attention to being twins. It's kind of a nonissue with us. We're individuals. We just do what we do and think what we think. Being twins is just a coincidence, like having the same color hair." Such twins stake their whole sense of identity on difference. They consider themselves individuals who happen to be twins. They feel indifferent toward their status as twins.

As you might imagine, however, the situation isn't quite so simple. Nontwins experience plenty of competition; why should these twins be exempt? When rivalry and outright hostility are evident (as they often are), it's hard to imagine that twinship isn't a primary factor. In fact, twins who claim indifference to being twins are usually putting a lot of energy into ignoring their situation. And it takes a *lot* of energy to do so. How can you ignore the fact that you were born into a unique sibling relationship? That you have shared your mother's womb with another person? Only twins, triplets, and other multiples have that experience. The impact can't possibly be insignificant. It's far more worthwhile to acknowledge the significance and to deal with its advantages and disadvantages than to negate its consequences.

Twins who have forged a bond of indifference, like the others I've discussed, also have a characteristic role, which might be labeled Not Twins at All—Just Two Individuals. This role essentially ignores—even excludes—the notion of twinship. It stresses individuality altogether over twindividuality. Although this role allows each twin the leeway for considerable independence, it can be problematic when the negative feelings of twinship are denied and avoided, for they do exist and do appear in adulthood.

Although twins may have separate friends and activities while growing up, and may act indifferent to being twins, negative feelings may exist. Cliff described how he and his brother Roy were "on separate tracks" as they grew up; neither paid much attention to the other. However, as Cliff and I explored his experiences as a twin, what stood out was an incident in which Roy had thrown a rock at Cliff for no reason and struck him in the head. Cliff wrote this off as "boy's play." But in fact it was an expression of rivalry inherent in their twinship. As a result, it's important to try to be aware of negative feelings that may exist; without acknowledging their existence, it can be difficult to move beyond them.

A fourth type of twins slug out the issue of sibling rivalry. For them, rivalry means all-out competition. "How good I am" equals "how much better I am than *you*." Twins such as these often compete on external issues—who's better academically or socially. When they grow up it becomes who gets married first, who has more money, who has more children. For example, Nina and Nancy would frequently argue over who weighed more. Weight became a form of competition. Being thinner gave one twin a pretext for claiming that she was better. Their weight difference was, in fact, the only thing that distinguished them.

The characteristic roles for competitive twins are what I call Good Twin/Bad Twin. Not only do the twins go in their own directions but these directions are diametrically opposed. Somehow a good-bad polarity gets established. One twin is the Little Angel; the other is the Troublemaker. Precisely because one twin behaves well, the other behaves badly. Self-definition becomes a matter of either-or.

One young twin I worked with was a classic instance of the Good Twin/Bad Twin syndrome. Alicia envied her sister Emilia; everything came easily to her. Emilia had a nicer car, better grades, prettier clothes. Alicia felt she could never measure up to her twin. So she didn't try; instead, she became the Bad Twin to Emilia's Good Twin— the ne'er-do-well, the troublemaker, the malcontent. As a Bad Twin, Alicia did whatever was the opposite of what Emilia did. She became good at being bad. This is a common situation. Bad Twins do everything badly and get into trouble. They never live up to their parents' expectations. As they get older and start dating, they pick partners who chagrin their parents.

Eventually Bad Twins must deal with their troubles. If they can understand their role and what it means, they can begin to let it go. They can learn that they don't really need to have everything against them to be recognized as having an identity.

These four kinds of twin bonds underscore once again the importance of identity in siblinghood. For twins the question of identity is, if anything, even more conspicuous than for nontwins.

Much of the psychological literature suggests that twins experience negative influences in developing an identity as a consequence of their powerful experience of shared parental attention. However, the most recent research (my own included) finds that being a twin and having an impaired sense of identity do not correlate. We can state at this point that twins' relationships and the qualities of the twin bond *do* influence their sense of individuality within a relationship, but not necessarily in a negative way.

What is not well documented, though, is how the positive aspects of twinship may help the forging of identity. It's possible that the companionship that twins have actually fosters personal security during times of family upheaval and change. Under such circumstances, the twin bond may be a powerful stabilizing force and a compensatory factor. For instance, Mark and Murray were adopted at birth but (unlike many twins) kept together. They constantly feel grateful for their good fortune. Doreen and her twin sister Danielle's parents divorced when the girls were very young. For many years after the divorce, Doreen and Danielle got shuttled from one relative to another until they finally settled down with an uncle and aunt. The twins felt tremendous mutual reassurance during this time; they provided a stabilizing force for each other.

Siblings of Twins

All the other siblings in a family will be affected by twins' special needs and demands. On the most fundamental level, this is a question of parental resources. Most parents greet the birth of twins with joy, but even the most thoroughly delighted parents will find the arrival of two babies at once a stressful event. The other siblings will almost certainly experience a diminishment of parental attention. In addition, twins are almost always a focus of attention for other relatives, family friends, and even total strangers may attend to the twins in ways and to a degree well out of keeping with what the other children experience—even more so than when a single baby arrives because of the sense of novelty and delight that twins evoke.

For older siblings, the twins may seem like the ultimate interlopers. Here they anticipated the arrival of a competitor only to encounter two at once! Sisters and brothers may feel tremendous resentment toward the twins' special status. Such a situation may lower the non-twins' self-esteem. They may feel less remarkable, less appreciated, less loved than before. They may respond to this drop in self-esteem by expressing their resentment toward the twins.

Evelyn describes her treatment from an older sister in these terms: "My twin and I were treated very badly by our older sister. She shut us out. After we grew up, she indicated that she was jealous of us and that's why she treated us so badly." She adds, "Parents need to be more aware of the brothers and sisters who are in the same family as twins. They need to educate the siblings about the uncontrollable closeness of the twins." This can be very helpful—for parents not only to learn about the dynamics of twinship but for them to help their other children understand the impact of twinship as well.

Younger nontwin siblings, may feel that they can never measure up to the twins. Perhaps even more intensely than older siblings, young siblings of twins may feel jealous, deprived, and resentful that the twins receive so much more attention. As a result, they may try to engage in activities at which they can excel. For example, Morgan, the younger brother of Dan and Drew, felt so inferior to the twins that even as a child he strenuously pursued a sports career and by adolescence, was a star baseball player. He worked doubly hard to keep up with his double brothers.

When there is only one sister or brother in addition to the twins, the "extra" sibling may end up feeling like a fifth wheel. The parents have each other. The twins have each other. But the other sibling has no relationship like the mutual exclusivity and emotional closeness either of marriage or of twinship.

If you're a brother or sister of twins whose childhood and adolescence included long-term sibling battles and hard feelings, or if you feel guilty about old conflicts with your twin siblings, it's possible to heal the wounds. Likewise, if you are a twin who feels bruised by hard times with nontwin siblings, you can soothe residual bad feelings.

First, you should think through your formative years and how they've influenced you. Just as twins often fail to appreciate the impact of twin status on their identities, you may not appreciate the impact of having been the brother or sister of twins. You may not recognize how your feelings toward the twins originated in their special bond and its effects on your whole family. Precisely because twinship drains so much energy from a mother and father, you may have felt that you weren't getting enough attention; and perhaps you weren't. But only by bringing these feelings into your full awareness can you come to terms with them.

It may be helpful to develop an understanding of what the twins experienced as well. Although your twin siblings may have acted as if they had it all, they went through hard times as well. As one nontwin said after gaining a better insight into twins, "I only started to understand what being a twin was like when I attended a twins' convention with my twin sisters." Many brothers and sisters come to understand their twin siblings better when they gain more awareness of the many elements that influence a family with twins. These elements are unavoidably vivid at a convention with five hundred sets of twins in attendance.

Adult twins too have unresolved feelings—for instance, guilt over how they treated their other siblings or anger over how the other siblings treated them. You may start to realize that your brothers' and sisters' taunts, insults, or mockery had nothing to do with you personally: rather, they happened because you came into the world *with someone else*—an ally from the start. And the twin "team" was too much (*two* much) for your sisters and brothers to handle. How did they respond? By trying to make you and your twin more manageable; by diminishing you. Unfortunately, their means of reduction may have diminished your sense of self-worth.

Stella, now thirty-nine years old, still struggles with the consequences of how her older sister treated her and her twin sister, Paula: "Agatha treated us terribly—'You're so ugly,' she'd say. 'You're so weird.'—all our lives, from the time we were babies up till the time she left home. I think she brought our self-esteem down a lot." Perhaps not surprisingly, Stella and Paula discovered at some point why Agatha treated them so badly. As Stella puts it, "At one family event— it was New Year's—Agatha told us that she was always jealous of us. We were shocked at that—we'd had no idea till that moment. We were probably thirty, and she was thirty-four. All those years we just had no idea."

13

Twins Grown Up

Twinship is siblinghood in overdrive—an even more complex and powerful experience than what other sisters and brothers have during childhood. The same holds true during adulthood. As Monica describes her relationship with Marianne, her identical twin: "It's been very hard because we have a constant need for each other—but that need is also a burden." Precisely because of this complexity and power, the difficulty of separation is unavoidable for adult twins.

Every child faces the task of separation from his or her parents and siblings. Because twinship is so intense, however, the issues of separation for twins are even more challenging. Twins must develop and maintain their identity in conjunction with someone whose physical resemblance and shared personal history make separating all the more complex.

For many twins, the first real separation occurs after leaving high school. Despite having experienced brief times apart in school or other settings, only after high school does the occasion arise for a prolonged physical separation. Going off to college, starting a job, or getting married all necessitate a considerable degree of separation.

A vivid example is Lois's experience. Her twin sister, Lynn, was distraught about Lois's wedding plans. Not only was Lois getting married but, of course, she was moving out of the room the twins had shared since birth. At one point, in a fit of anger, Lynn broke up the sisters' record collection. This act was symbolic of what Lynn felt was happening. In her eyes, the twinship itself was being broken up.

The Ambivalence of Separation

Whatever propels twins toward separation from each other, the decision to move off on one's own is often complex and conflicted. For many twins, wanting to move out of the twin orbit evokes guilt. Sometimes the changes they are undergoing can make them feel as if they are abandoning their sister or brother—especially if the twin says so outright. Such expressions can heighten one's anger at being depended on in frustrating ways.

Ryan, for instance, came to me for therapy because he felt guilty about the changes taking place in his relationship with his twin, Ray. Ryan, engaged to a woman named Janet, spent far more time with Janet than with Ray. This situation caused double guilt for Ryan. Not only was Ryan with his brother less than before, but Ryan also knew that, since he was the more gregarious twin, Ray now felt socially adrift. Ryan worried that he was abandoning his brother. At the same time, he expressed an understandable desire to get on with life and his relationship with Janet. Ryan's ambivalence about separating from his brother ultimately prolonged his engagement to Janet for six years, till he worked through these issues.

If you are a twin who wants separation, start by developing a little empathy toward your twin. He or she has shared something special with you since before birth and has come to depend on you. Although you may feel ready to try swimming on your own, your twin may feel too shaky to do the same. If you can express empathy rather than anger, you may be able to find ways of getting together so that you're more at ease in sharing. Just as you're making yourself less available, you can make a point of letting your twin know when you *are* available. It's a matter of reshaping time together rather than rejecting your twin.

Admittedly, it's hard to appreciate how your twin may be feeling when you want to pursue your own interests and desires. However, sometimes understanding your twin's view can make you more sensitive to the changes you're both undergoing. Talking over the situation can go a long way in easing the tensions. Specifically, making it clear that you're still available can allay many fears.

I frequently work with twins on this issue of separation, helping them manage the many negative feelings they experience as they move toward their own independent lives. They are often terribly troubled by anxiety and guilt about going off alone. Sometimes twins argue as they respond to the changes they're making. Many times their anxiety and guilt are so strong that twins are inclined to relinquish whatever goals they're pursuing—a job, a relationship, an education. But these goals are of great importance. I encourage them to continue with their plans.

It is most important to remember this: however difficult this process may be, inhibiting yourself will do both of you a disservice. Limiting your own education, social development, or breadth of interest will make you angry and resentful in the long run. You'll feel (as one of my patients put it) "pulled down" by your twin—which is not good for either of you. You have to learn to emerge from the *merge* that you and your twin have shared. If you can keep this in mind and accept that you may feel some discomfort in the short run, you'll both feel happier and more fulfilled in the longer term. You may not be entwined, but you'll still be twinned.

Many twins can appreciate that a sister or brother wants a more separate life—college, marriage, or some other change—yet they still feel left behind. Your feeling of abandonment is understandable; however, you're facing an opportunity to begin to grow on your own as well. If you can build enjoyable activities, events, and experiences into your life, you'll feel stronger in your individuality. If too much of your sense of self has been invested in your twindividuality, it's time to develop more of a balance. Doing so will make you stronger, not weaker.

For example, Doug came to me for treatment because he felt anxious when his twin brother got married. He worried about making his life work out as he'd always planned. We worked on developing his own interests and activities. In time, Doug became more independent—less focused on his twin as the organizing principle of his life.

If you are feeling abandoned or resentful of your twin's separate activities, appreciate your emotions. This is a big transition. Being aware of how connected you are to your twin, and of how strongly you'll be affected when that contact changes, can help you deal positively with the situation.

When Twins Marry

Marriage automatically alters the twin bond in some way. Twinship can be so intense that, despite its genuine delights, some twins need a way to back off from their constant closeness. Sometimes one twin will find a romantic partner as a means of moving out of the twin orbit. Occasionally, this push occurs in the twins' teens and leads to marriage. Ursula, for instance, is an identical twin who met Ted when they were both eighth-graders. Ursula and Ted dated through high school and married soon after graduation. Similarly, an identical twin named Meg met Keith at the age of thirteen, dated him till right after high school, and married him.

It's not unusual for one twin to want to move beyond the twin orbit sooner than the other. Even if this doesn't occur during the teen years, it may occur when one twin feels ready to get married. One twin's decision to marry can be very upsetting for the other twin, who feels threatened or abandoned. Because twinship is so close a relationship in its own right, many twins have intense and mixed feelings about getting married, since marriage both offers an opportunity to pursue their independent relationship and entails an intense separation from their twin. As Mel said, "I felt that, to get married, I'd have to go through a divorce first."

The story of Carlie and Carl is a particularly dramatic illustration of the pressures one twin may feel when the other marries. Carlie and Carl are fraternal twins who have always been very close. Carlie was

very distressed when her brother got married; she felt not only abandoned but replaced as well because Carl was marrying someone who
looked exactly like her and was also named Carlie. The only way she
felt able to preserve her identity was to legally change her name. When
Carlie came to me for therapy, she showed me a picture of herself
with her brother and his new wife, and she asked, "Who do you think
the twins are? My sister-in-law and I look more alike than my brother
and I do!"

Another common scenario is that when one twin falls in love and
gets married, the other rapidly follows suit. On the one hand, this
quick follow-up redresses the imbalance created when only one is
married. On the other hand, this sequence can seem intrusive.

Rachel, for instance, has always been involved with her twin sister,
Rebecca; they have shared everything; they have defined everything in
terms of equality. Now Rachel is getting married, leaving her job and
her family, and moving out of state. The struggle for Rachel is that
she feels guilty about pursuing her individual plans. About the time
that Rachel started to arrange her wedding, Rebecca met someone at
a party, started dating him, and is now talking about getting married.
In therapy sessions, Rachel expresses her anger that Rebecca has co-
opted all Rachel's wedding plans. "I'm looking at this bride's magazine
and Rebecca takes it away to look at dresses for herself!" Having
shared everything with her twin all their lives, Rachel can't even have
her wedding to herself.

When Vicki got engaged to marry, her twin sister, Nicki, started
dating a man and soon became engaged as well. Nicki worried, however, that announcing her engagement shortly before Vicki's wedding,
as she planned, would rain on her sister's parade. Nicki decided,
however, that since she and Vicki were twins, and since their lives
already had a certain symmetry, she would go ahead and make her
announcement as she wished.

Sometimes one twin marries and the other doesn't, but the unmarried twin moves nearer to the newly married twin. This enables the
twins to remain connected despite leading more independent lives
than before.

Sometimes a twin chooses to stay unmarried out of ambivalence over entering a new relationship based on sharing (that is, marriage) after so many years of participating in a relationship also based on sharing. Either this twin's loyalty remains totally focused on the twin bond or he or she wants a respite from this sort of interaction.

A pair of twins who came to me for therapy had always done everything together. Their lives had been equal from Day One. Since childhood they'd played with the same toys, worn the same sorts of clothes, gone the same places, eaten the same kinds of food. For them, being equal was the highest good. The problem now was that they had entered adolescence. They wanted to date. Unfortunately, they'd taken equality to a complicated further step: they both wanted to date the same girl. All kinds of misunderstandings and difficulties ensued.

How did the twins resolve this problem? Since they didn't want to share the girl they loved, they decided that neither of them would date. The push toward intimacy with other people bumped headlong into their long-standing allegiance to each other. Since they couldn't easily find other twins to date, and the absence of other twins might have left them either competing over the same girl or imbalanced in their commitments (one of them involved, the other not), they decided to relinquish romantic involvement at this time. Some twins, such as Ed and Eliott, who work together and find that their work consumes much of their time and energy, may also decide not to marry.

In short, twinship involves such a constant experience of sharing that sometimes one twin or both elect not to separate or go through the further experience of sharing that marriage requires.

Another solution to the issue of separation and the marital quandary it evokes is to marry other twins. Such twins have a real investment in twindividuality and in keeping things balanced between them. Marriage becomes an opportunity to share equally yet again. This can become an ideal arrangement for twins who have a strong bond of equality.

If you aren't a twin, you might imagine that twins marrying twins would create all sorts of tensions and misunderstandings. In fact, twin-to-twin marriages often work very well. They reflect such a premium on twinship and on keeping the bonds strong that there's a constant expression of mutual commitment. At times the level of sharing is almost incomprehensible to nontwins. While this is a rare marital arrangement, and statistics on these marriages are difficult to come by, research suggests that there are approximately seventy sets of twins married to other twins in the United States. The ten sets of twins married to other twins with whom I've spoken personally have all expressed how pleased they are with their marital arrangements, which allow them both the intimacy of marriage and the intimacy of twinship.

A variation on these themes occurs when a twin from one set finds a twin from another set for his or her partner. Sometimes an identical twin marries another identical twin, which affords each of them the opportunity to create another twinship.

Each of these variations on marriage choices for twins evolves from the issue of separation and forging a new relationship. Each twin in a pair will approach this milestone with different feelings. Some will be eager, others will be more reluctant, but twinship will affect the marital experience, which will alter the twin bond. That bond may be replicated in the marriage and contribute to harmony or conflict.

If you are a twin and are married, the most helpful thing you can do to enhance your marriage is to recognize the importance of your twin status. Reflect on how you feel about being a twin. Do you highlight it? Minimize it? Negate that it has any significance whatsoever? The different types of twin bonds—equality, complementarity, indifference, and competition—affect twins' marriages and provide a way of identifying several important influences on twins as they move toward interpersonal commitment and marriage.

Bennett expected his wife, Bonnie, to share all her resources with him so that things would be even between them. He expected her to pay his expenses, since she had more money than he did. He also expected her to take care of the children and the house, since he believed she had more free time. Bonnie felt these expectations were unfair and burdensome. In fact, Bennett's expectations had their roots in his relationship with Bernard, his twin brother, with whom Bennett had a totally equal relationship. If he or his brother ever had more than the other, they'd always shared it to even things out.

Alan and Sherrie have always thought of themselves as an odd couple. Alan is artistic, emotionally restless, and bohemian in both appearance and behavior—an accomplished poet and playwright who calls himself a "literary troublemaker." Sherrie is a respected sociologist but also much more domestic than her husband. She prides herself not only on the rigor of her research but also on the beauty of her home and the excellence of her cooking. Together, Alan and Sherrie sometimes seem oddly matched, yet they have a close marriage and a strong sense of each other as "opposite sides of a coin." In fact, their marriage echoes many aspects of Alan's relationship with Andy, his identical twin brother. While they were growing up, Andy was always the stable, rational homebody; Alan was the temperamental artist. The brothers seemed to complement each other—a balancing act that stabilized their relationship as twins. Now Alan has found a similar bond in Sherrie: the perfect balance to his intense mind and tumultuous emotions.

Gerald could no longer tolerate his wife's indifference to him. Catherine would stay late at work night after night; sometimes she'd even stay out with friends without letting Gerald know her whereabouts. If things didn't change, Gerald wanted to end the marriage. It turned out that Catherine was an identical twin who placed no importance on her twin status. Since she hadn't spoken to her sister (toward whom she felt a deep rage) for many years, Catherine claimed that her twinship was irrelevant to her. Her continuing anger at her twin, however, suggested otherwise. Catherine was angry precisely because her sister treated her with great indifference. For instance, Catherine heard about her sister's car accident from their mother. Catherine's sister had never bothered calling to let Catherine know what had happened or whether she was all right. It was not surprising that Catherine duplicated this indifference in her manner toward Gerald, even to the point of neglecting to phone him of her whereabouts.

When Don and Belle came to me for treatment, they had two matched complaints. Belle complained that Don never acknowledged her; Don complained that Belle was always crowding his "space." An additional complaint was that in this couple's work together (they are both architects), Belle resented Don's tendency to ridicule her ideas, then claim them for his own. Belle felt exhausted from what she regarded as her husband's constant efforts to undermine and outdo her. When I inquired into their background, I discovered not only that Don was a fraternal twin but also that he had an extremely rivalrous relationship with his brother. He had no insight, however, into how competitively he behaved toward his twin.

These four examples suggest how twin status, combined with each of the characteristic twin bonds, can affect marriage. Bennett came to appreciate that his notion of the "fair share" was different from Bonnie's. With that recognition, he was able to redefine his own concept of sharing and thus redefine his household and financial responsibilities.

Alan and Sherrie's situation presented the most strengths of the four I've mentioned here. They have their ups and downs, but there's a fairly stable rhythm to their life together. This is not surprising. In general, the bond of complementarity is most conducive to a positive rapport between marriage partners. (This phenomenon shows up in other situations. For instance, married couples often parcel out tasks, activities, and interests in a similar fashion. "We pool our resources," some couples say. "You handle the money; I'll take care of the social network." The French psychologist Rene Zazzo calls this the Couple Effect: a means of maintaining balance within a relationship by distributing tasks and benefits between the partners.) However, one negative aspect of complementarity is that one twin may function in the classic role of the Good Twin while the other assumes the role of the Bad Twin. In marriage, this can manifest itself as one partner always claiming to be right while the other always feels he or she is in the wrong. So far, Alan and Sherrie have avoided this trap.

Catherine's twin bond had clearly a powerful impact on her marriage. As Catherine began to see how old indifference and repressed anger toward her sister was ruining her marriage, she could start to understand the situation. Gerald and Catherine are still at work repairing their bond.

Finally, I helped Don and Belle see how Don's twin status—and most important his bond of competition with his brother—had set up patterns that the couple had replicated. Don's behavior was understandable but potentially damaging to his marriage. By grasping the legacies of his sibling rivalry, however, Don could start to short-circuit his old competitive impulses. Moreover, these realizations helped Belle to see why Don needed more "space."

It's hard to overestimate the significance of what you've experienced as a twin. Sharing space in your mother's womb; sharing your birthday; sharing (if you're an identical twin) your physical features; sharing parental attention; sharing the world's fascination with you—the cumulative effect of such intense, constant sharing can't help but influence the quality of your interpersonal relationships. The effects may be both positive and negative, but they will be there.

Many twins are asked, "How does it feel to be a twin?" Often they respond, "It's all I know." For twins, being a twin is a given. If you're a twin, realize that, although it's all you know, it's as critical to your identity and how you view yourself as being male or female is, and it will consequently affect all your interpersonal relationships as well.

For this reason, I suggest, to the degree possible, that you try to appreciate that your twin status confers a unique experience on you. This in turn brings along an intensity and multiplicity of feelings that have shaped how you become involved with other people. Being a twin will sometimes facilitate an immediate, intense, empathic, sense of connectedness with other people; at other times, being a twin may engender intense rivalrous feelings toward others. By beginning to reflect on your twin bond and on how you and your twin arrived long ago at a mutual balance, you will gain some insight into how you position yourself with other people as well.

In addition to how the twin bond affects a marriage, all the other issues that affect marriage—among them jealousy, competition, and rivalry—come into play for twins as well. All marital partners expect to be Number One with their mate. However, twins have already forged a partnership with each other. Because the twin still expects to be Number One in his or her twin's eyes after that twin's marriage, expectations may come into conflict. In twins' marriages, jealousy (both twin-to-twin and twin-to-partner) is common. For these reasons, the issue of exclusivity in marriage is even more complex and intense for twins than it is for nontwins.

When a Twin Dies

One final aspect of separation that occurs in twinship—one nobody chooses—is when a twin dies. Whether the death occurs as a consequence of accident, illness, or even suicide, the anguish it evokes is enormous. The death of a twin not only takes the twin away but also extinguishes the twin bond. The surviving twin becomes a solo twin. As one of my patients described it, "I feel as if I've lost part of my soul." This loss also calls the surviving twin's sense of identity into question. "We were The Twins," said Renee, who lost her identical twin sister, "but who am I now?" The surviving twin faces the challenge of an altered duality: to live life both as a twin and as a nontwin.

The magnitude of this loss is often underestimated by virtually everyone—sometimes even the surviving twin. Yet its impact is tremendous. When Joshua's brother died, for instance, he said, "I could live with the death of my children or even my wife, but the death of my twin feels like an amputation." Harriet expressed her loss in these terms: "Losing my twin sister, Henrietta, was unbearable. I felt guilty that I didn't feel so bad when my mother or father died because my twin was still alive then. She was my sense of family."

The death of a twin means the loss of what many twins have experienced as an ever-present companion. This companionship encompasses the sense of unconditional availability from a friend who is totally understanding and completely accepting. As Trish put it, "I can never again walk into a room and know that, without my saying a word, I am completely accepted." Henry's situation provides another striking instance: his identical twin brother has been dead for forty years, yet Henry still feels an acute sense of loss. He says, "It's not the absence of the twin that's painful but rather what has gone out of the surviving twin."

Here are some guidelines for dealing with the death of a twin. The most important thing to realize is that there is no timetable for grief. Many people will offer well-intended comments such as "Don't worry—you'll be over it soon." But such remarks can inadvertently make dealing with the loss more difficult: if you have lost your twin, sentiments such as these may prompt you to feel there's something wrong with you for not getting over your loss more quickly. You need to understand that people really do not grasp the depth of your loss precisely because they don't grasp the nature of being a twin. Don't expect that they will. This is one of the most difficult aspects of what twins encounter when their twin dies, that people expect their grief to diminish in a timely way. It doesn't. As one twin put it, "It doesn't ever go away. You just learn to live with it."

Second, accept that no one can replace your twin. That's okay. The reality is that your twin was, and is, irreplaceable.

Just as important is pacing yourself. You're going to go through a period of intense anger. You may find yourself blaming everyone around you or feeling angry about their lack of understanding. You may continue to experience tremendous sadness, emptiness, loneliness, and heartache. As Angela said, "Antonia and I used to spend Sundays together. Now it's a big void."

You may find yourself feeling emotionally depleted and physically exhausted. You may be unable to give to other people, whether your children, spouse, friends, or others. Try to appreciate your pain. Set limits for yourself so that you pace your exertions and replenish your energies. Doris used to snap at her children when she felt worn out and unable to respond to their needs. Her impatience made her feel terribly guilty. Doris now realizes that she simply runs out of steam at times. She accepts that when it happens, rather than expecting herself to carry on. As a result, she is able to give both her husband and her children clear messages that contain her limits, such as "I can't do this for you now, but I'll get to it later." She no longer feels guilty about taking care of herself.

Depending on the circumstances of your twin's death, be aware that coping with someone else's illness may evoke the old feelings about losing your twin. For instance, Esther's friend Vincent recently had a stroke. As much as she wanted to help him recuperate, she felt flooded by memories of her twin sister's battle with cancer, which made it extremely difficult for her as she helped her friend convalesce. The usual stresses of life, including illness, cannot only become amplified themselves because of what you experienced but also trigger old pain and sadness about the loss of your twin.

Finding a way of keeping your twin's memory alive for yourself may help you deal with these feelings. This is especially true on the practical level: coping with your twin's clothes, birthdays, and holidays. Some have found that by wearing a particular item of clothing, they can keep their twin with them. Others have found that holding on to items of furniture or personal effects serves the same purpose. Some have described experiencing a psychic connection to their twin. For instance, Audrey feels that whenever the light in the closet goes on without her husband or Audrey herself having hit the switch, it's her twin's presence. If you have this experience, don't be surprised; it isn't uncommon.

Finally, if you are an identical twin, be aware of this possibility as well: Some people may mistake you for the twin who died. When this occurs, you may feel a tremendous feeling of sadness and loss. Depending on how close you were to your twin, such feelings are almost inevitable.

I have a therapy group of patients who have lost their twins. They have found these five coping guidelines extremely useful in dealing with the sense of loss that follows a twin's death, as well as managing the feelings that arise as they deal with friends, family, and people at work. These and other solo twins often feel not only sadness, abandonment, and anger but also relief and guilt. Some twins, who have felt burdened by their twinship now feel relief at their freedom; at the same time, they feel guilty precisely about this sense of relief. Both the relief and the guilt are normal responses to loss. If you find yourself in a similar situation, just realize that your grief brings with it all these mixed feelings, and that you can take as long as you may need to sort through them.

The complexity of separation in its many forms along with the intensity of feelings that twins experience make twinship a mixed blessing. In sharing so much, twins gain in abundance, but they can also experience great loss.

14

Conclusion

Throughout this book we've looked at the array of forces that create conflicts—from day-to-day difficulties to more acute problems—that hamper relationships between sisters and brothers. My intentions have been to give you a clearer understanding of what your sibling relationships are about and to help you gain at least six insights that will enhance your ability to shape these relationships more positively.

First, recognize that, despite its origins in your past, sibling rivalry endures long past childhood. You have carried old roles away from your family experience—roles that may be either positive or negative and that can perpetuate competition and hostility between you and your siblings. If you were a kid brother and felt your siblings looked down on you, this role may be operating even now. Seeing roles in this light may help you understand the situation, not feel so belittled, and change the way you respond rather than react.

Second, the best way to get a handle on your sibling relationships is to clarify your own ideal of siblinghood. How are you pursuing your ideal of the Good-Enough Sibling? How are you inadvertently taking on aspects of the Supersibling role? Are you making yourself available to such an extent that you place no limits on your emotions, time, and resources? Are you more intricately involved in your sister's or brother's life than is appropriate for either of you? Or are you able to be comfortable as a Good-Enough Sibling instead? To clarify your ideal of siblinghood, you must evaluate your old expectations and see them as part of the past; you must perceive your brothers, your sisters, and yourself not in terms of who you were as children but in terms of who you are as adults.

Third, setting limits provides you with a method for dealing with each of these issues. If you can set limits with your siblings, you can increase the likelihood of having more positive, loving relationships with them; you can also preempt some of the problems described in this book. Setting limits is not just a technique for containing a brother's or sister's demands on you. It's also a way to redefine the boundaries of your relationship. After all, becoming a Good-Enough Sibling means not only changing your expectations but also using the available tools to make these expectations clear.

Fourth, I hope those of you who are caught up in cold war conflicts or have had to back off from a sibling relationship can understand the dynamics of what has gone on in your relationship. The techniques described in this book should help you to turn down the heat so you can stay involved with your sisters or brothers despite your conflicts. Perhaps you can provide a context or "frame" for your conflict so that it's not such a total rupture. Perhaps you can learn to say, "Look, let's cool it for the time being, and let's come back when we're both a little bit less emotional about this." A break in communication doesn't have to be harsh or permanent.

Fifth, once you recognize that you are still dealing with unresolved feelings toward your sisters and brothers, you can better understand how these emotions may transform other important people in your life into Invisible Siblings. This recognition will help you see how you may have not only direct difficulties with your sisters and brothers but may also be dealing with Invisible Siblings in terms of problems that are a more indirect offshoot of sibling relationships. These problems may involve your in-laws, co-workers, or others. Such problems generally involve either your own or another person's unresolved sibling issues. This book can provide you with the means to take the "pulse" of these issues and identify what they are about. Ideally, you can then begin relating to your in-laws, co-workers, or friends in a different manner—one unburdened by sibling dynamics.

Sixth, keep in mind that major life events, such as a marriage or the death of a parent, can have far greater significance to you and your siblings than you may imagine. If you can maintain an awareness of the power such events have over you, your sisters, and your brothers, you may be able to save a sibling relationship under stress or even rebuild the foundation for one that suffered earlier damage.

Finally, if you are a twin, you're going to experience an intensity of feelings that can heighten sibling rivalry. The twin bond in its several forms characterizes the nature of the twin relationship and is important because it may be replicated in other key relationships, especially marriage. Remember that if you are a twin, reflecting on your twin status can help you get a fuller sense of yourself and the various roles you may have acquired that have contributed to your identity. This is especially significant if you are married.

Siblinghood is powerful. It has the potential for filling our lives with delight, amusement, reassurance, and consolation; anger, bafflement, and exasperation; companionship or loneliness; the warmest friendship or the coldest enmity. For most people, siblinghood is a mix of experiences, some of which can create both internal and external conflict.

However, you have at least the potential to define how this power affects you. This is not to say that you can remake your sisters or brothers. Neither does it mean that you can transform your relationships with them from frustrating to delightful simply by force of will. It does mean, however, that you can decide what kind of sibling you want to be and, by this means, influence the nature of the relationship you have with your brothers and sisters.

Bibliography

Allen, M. G., S. I. Greenspan, and William Pollin. "The Effects of Parental Perceptions on Early Development of Twins," in *Annual Progress in Child Psychiatry and Child Development*, 1977, 305–315.

Arnstein, Helene S. *Brothers and Sisters/Sisters and Brothers*. New York: E. P. Dutton, 1979.

Atkins, Dale V. *Sisters*. New York: Arbor House, 1984.

Bank, Stephen P., and Michael D. Kahn. *The Sibling Bond*. New York: Basic Books, 1982.

Burlingham, D. T. "The Relationship of Twins to Each Other," in *The Psychoanalytic Study of the Child*, 1949, Vol. 3/4, 57–72.

Cassill, Kay. *Twins: Nature's Amazing Mystery*. New York: Atheneum, 1982.

Donnelly, Katherine F. *Recovering from the Loss of a Sibling*. New York: Dodd, Mead, 1988.

Dunn, Judy, and Carole Kendrick. *Siblings: Love, Envy, and Understanding*. Cambridge, Mass.: Harvard University Press, 1982.

Dunn, Judy, and Robert Plomin. *Separate Lives: Why Siblings Are So Different*. New York: Basic Books, 1990.

Fishel, Elizabeth. *Sisters: Love and Rivalry Inside the Family and Beyond*. New York: Quill, 1979.

Hift, K. "An Experimental Study of the Twinning Reaction and Ego Development," in *University Microfilm International*, 1980, Ann Arbor, Mich.

Hirt, E. J. "Separation-Individual in Twins: An Objective Assessment," in *University Microfilms International*, 1980, Ann Arbor, Mich.

Hoopes, Margaret, and James M. Harper. *Birth Order Roles and Sibling Patterns in Individual and Family Therapy*. Rockville, Md.: Aspen Publishers, 1987.

Jarrett, D. B., and Maureen McGarty. "Twin Yearning," in *The Hillside Journal of Clinical Psychiatry*, 1980, Vol. 2, No. 2, 86–90.

Kahn, Michael D., and Karen Gail Lewis. *Siblings in Therapy: Lifespan and Clinical Issues*. New York: W. W. Norton, 1988.

Koch, Helen. *Twins and Twin Relationships*. Chicago: University of Chicago, 1966.

Lassers, Elizabeth, and Robert Nordon. "Separation-Individuation of an Identical Twin," in *Adolescent Psychiatry*, 1978, Vol. 6, 469–479.

Leman, Kevin. *The Birth Order Book*. New York: Dell, 1985.

Leman, Kevin. *Growing Up Firstborn*. New York: Dell, 1989.

Leonard, M. R. "Problems in Identification and Ego Development in Twins," in *Psychoanalytic Study of the Child*, 1961, Vol. 16, 300–320.

McDermott, John. *The Complete Book on Sibling Rivalry*. New York: Perigee, 1980.

Maenchen, Anna. "Object Cathoxis is a Borderline Twin," in *Psychoanalytic Study of the Child*, 1968, Vol. 23, 438–456.

Mendelson, Morton J. *Becoming a Brother*. Cambridge, Mass.: MIT Press, 1990.

Orr, D. W. "A Psychoanalytic Study of a Fraternal Twin," in *Psychoanalytic Quarterly*, 1941, Vol. 1, 284–296.

Ortmeyer, D. H. "The We-self of Identical Twins," *Contemporary Psychoanalysis*, 1970. Vol. 6, 125–142.

Siemon, Mari. "The Separation-Individuation Process in Adult Twins," in *American Journal of Psychotherapy.*, 1980, July, Vol. 34, 387–400.

Strean, Herbert S., and Lucy Freeman. *Raising Cain: How to Help Your Children Achieve a Happy Sibling Relationship*. New York: St. Martin's Press, 1988.

Terry, G. E. "The Separation-Individuation Process in Same Sex Twins: A Review of the Literature," in *Maternal Child Nursing Journal*, 1965, Vol. 4, 121–128.

Toman, Walter. *Family Constellation: Its Effects on Personality and Social Behavior.* New York: Springer, 1961.

Toman, Walter. *Family Therapy and Sibling Position.* Northvale, N. J.: Jason Aronson, 1988.

Wiehe, Vernon R. *Sibling Abuse: Hidden Physical, Emotional, and Sexual Trauma.* Lexington, Mass.: Lexington Books, 1990.

Zazzo, Rene. "Genesis and Peculiarities of the Personality of Twins," in W. E. Nance (ed.), *Twin Research, Part A: Psychology and Methodology.* New York: Alan Liss, 1978.

Acknowledgments

Like all complex endeavors, the process of writing this book has benefited from the ideas, insights, and experiences of many people. I want to thank all those who have been particularly helpful in bringing this project to completion, for they are the ones who have made this book happen.

First and foremost, I thank Marc Snowman—my husband, colleague, partner, and especially trusted friend and adviser. I am grateful for his intricate involvement and input on so many levels. It was invaluable.

I owe profound thanks as well to my dear friend Dr. Sonya Rhodes for her magnanimous heart and generous spirit. It was she who first made this book a possibility; at every later stage of the project, she offered her support, encouragement, and insight. Yet what I value most about her presence throughout the writing of *Adult Sibling Rivalry* is the gift of her friendship.

I also owe deep gratitude to my agent, Denise Marcil, who, because she is such an "ace" at what she does, was able to transform the initial idea for this book into a practical reality. She also advised and encouraged me throughout the process in her own perceptive ways.

I wish to thank Edward Myers—my partner in writing *Adult Sibling Rivalry*, and my Invisible Sibling—for his unwavering enthusiasm, relentless energy, talent for detail, flexibility, responsiveness, and for always going above and beyond the call of duty. He made writing this book my most personally enriching collaboration. Most of all, however, I want to thank him for his "word magic."

Jane Meara has been the ideal editor: constantly supportive yet ready with specific suggestions, comments, and ideas. Her superb style and keen insights on every level—from the intricacies of psychological theory to the fine points of English prose style—have enhanced the manuscript beyond calculation.

In addition, I wish to thank my colleagues and friends for what each has brought to the project. Dr. Cody Wilson, whose belief in the importance of sibling relationships opened the door to my research in this area, has, through his inimitable style as a researcher, left an unmistakable imprint on this project. My "sister of the heart" friend, Dr. Josie Palleja, was consistently supportive and helpful in every respect. Thanks for being with me every step of the way. To my M.T.A. friend, Kathy Pomerantz, I offer my forever thanks. As always, you brought your special touch to this book. My thanks also to Arden Greenspan-Goldberg, my "soul-sister," for all the spirit and encouragement you've given me. To Lynn Long and Lori Stewart I feel tremendous appreciation for their warm help. I'm also very grateful to all the wonderful twins of the International Twin Association for sharing their experiences with me. David Grand, my friend and (once again) technical adviser, provided his expert clinical insights. Dr. Louis Keith, Donald Keith, Pat Malmstrom, Nancy Rica Schiff, Dr. Jack Snowman, Dr. Richard April, Dr. Cheryl Futterman, and Dr. Raymond Brandt also provided help with my research.

My parents' ever-present love and support are vital forces in my life. I can't thank you enough. I'd like to thank my Aunt Ruth for being the first to say, "Why don't you write a book?"

Finally, I want to thank everyone who contributed his or her story to *Adult Sibling Rivalry*—my patients, my friends, and the many others who offered to be interviewed. They are ultimately the bedrock of my insights into siblinghood. I wish I could thank each of them individually; since that's not possible, let me say simply, "You know who you are, and your contributions have been immeasurable."

INDEX

221